THE DEVIL'S TRIANGLE

THE DEVIL'S TRIANGLE

by ELWOOD D. BAUMANN

Franklin Watts   New York   London   1976

To Bunny

Photographs courtesy of: The National Archives: p. x; U.S. Naval Photographic Center: pp. 4, 63, 69, 70; New York Public Library Picture Collection: pp. 24, 29; Atlantic Mutual Insurance Company: p. 42; U.S. Navy, Atlantic Fleet Photographic Center: p. 73; Smithsonian Institution: p. 90.

Book design by Rafael H. Hernandez

Library of Congress Cataloging in Publication Data
Baumann, Elwood D
  The Devil's Triangle.

  Bibliography: p.
  Includes index.
  SUMMARY: Recounts the many mysterious, unexplained losses of ships and planes in the area of the Atlantic Ocean between Florida and Bermuda.
  1. Bermuda Triangle—Juvenile literature. [1. Bermuda Triangle] I. Title.
G525.B36   910′.09′16363   75-22020
ISBN 0-531-01094-5

Copyright © 1976 by Elwood D. Baumann
All rights reserved
Printed in the United States of America
10 9 8 7

TABLE OF CONTENTS

	Author's Note	vii
I	Flight 19	1
II	The Devil's Triangle	16
III	The First Signs of Trouble	23
IV	The Disappearance of Theodosia Alston	32
V	The Saga of the *Mary Celeste*	39
VI	Joshua Slocum—an Unlikely Victim	53
VII	The Suspicious Case of the *Cyclops*	61
VIII	The *Carroll A. Deering*	76
IX	A Survivor Tells His Story	82
X	The *Star Tiger*	86
XI	Other Mysteries of the Air	93
XII	The U.S. Air Force vs. the Devil's Triangle	105
XIII	Questions Still Unanswered	109
	Bibliography	113
	Index	115

AUTHOR'S NOTE

On April 25, 1974, the author finished his first round of research for this book and prepared to leave Miami for his home in Spain. Before going out to the airport, he bought a copy of *The Miami News*. The headline on that day was—YACHT DISAPPEARS IN DEVIL'S TRIANGLE.

The *Saba Bank*, a fifty-four-foot yacht valued at $300,000, had been missing for six weeks. She had sailed from Nassau in the Bahamas on March 10. Her electronics equipment was the very best, but the Coast Guard had not been able to make contact with her. Neither had the Bahamas Air-Sea Rescue Association, which launched an intensive search. At the time this is being written, the fate of the *Saba Bank* is still unknown.

Not every boat or plane that disappears in the Devil's Triangle makes newspaper headlines. There is no way of knowing, in fact, just how many lives have been lost over the years. Neither is it possible to tell how many disappearances of light aircraft and smaller boats are due to negligence or ignorance.

It is evident, however, that a frighteningly high number of losses cannot be explained away. Neither negligence nor ignorance caused planes and ships manned by experienced crews to vanish without a trace.

It is this lack of rational explanation that gives the Devil's Triangle its treacherous reputation as well as its mysterious fascination.

Elwood Baumann

YACHT DISAPPEARS IN DEVIL'S TRIANGLE

Mystery Of Bermuda Triangle's Missing Ships

Where Disaster Means Mystery

SIX FEARED LOST IN "BERMUDA TRIANGLE"

THE ETERNAL DRAMA OF THE SEA

Mysteries Flood the Atlantic

WHERE DID THE SHIPS GO?

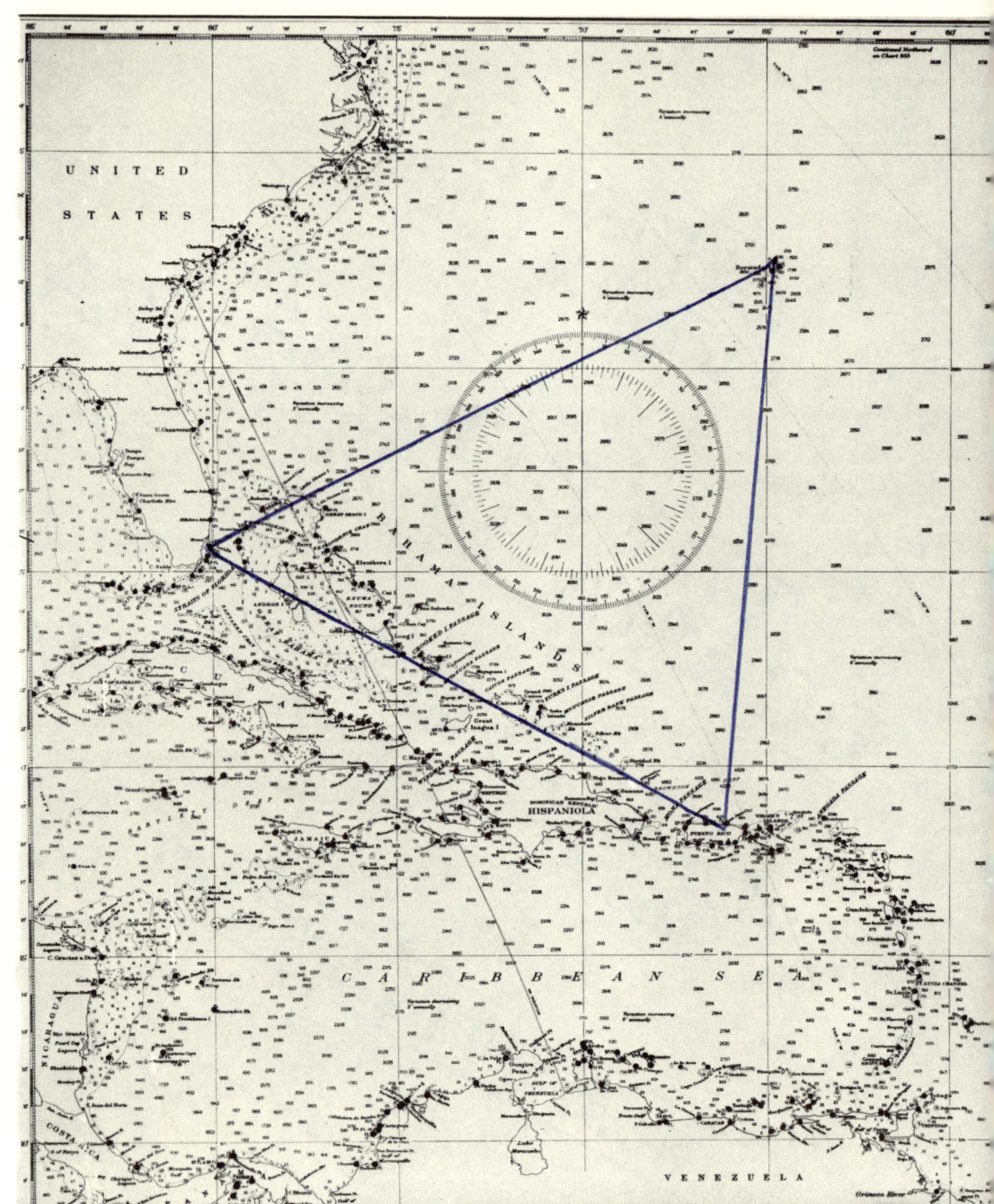

A mariner's map of the area known as the Devil's Triangle

Flight 19

The Florida skies were bright and clear on the afternoon of December 5, 1945. The Second World War had been over for nearly four months and many of the sailors and marines at the Fort Lauderdale Naval Air Station were awaiting discharge. One of them was Marine Sergeant Robert Gallivan of Northampton, Massachusetts.

"Well, this is my last flight today," Gallivan said to his buddies. "Tomorrow at this time, I'll be a civilian."

Private First Class Robert Gruebel of Long Island City, New York, looked up at the cloudless sky. "It's a nice day for flying," he said.

Gallivan and Corporal Allen Kosnar of Kenosha, Wisconsin, laughed good-humoredly. "Don't you ever think of anything except flying, Gruebel?" asked Gallivan.

"I like to fly," was the young aerial gunner's straightforward reply. Gruebel's love for airplanes had earned him the nickname of Yo-Yo. He flew whenever he had a chance. It made no difference to him what kind of plane it was or where it was going. If he could hitch a ride on it, he always did.

The routine flights out over the Atlantic bored Gallivan and Kosnar, but Gruebel found them wildly exciting. Strangely, though, the airman had no interest in becoming a pilot. When he finished his tour of duty in the Marine Air Force, he was going to go to divinity school and study to be a minister.

As far as Gallivan and Kosnar were concerned, the routine flights were about as exciting as lying on their bunks. Kosnar had been doing a lot of flying in the last few weeks and was tired of it. Gallivan had seen nearly three years of combat duty as an aerial gunner in the Pacific. He disliked the hops out over the Atlantic and was happy that he wouldn't have to make any more after the one today. He'd had all the time in the air that he wanted.

It was still early when the three friends got back to their barracks after lunch. They wouldn't have to report to the flight line for another hour.

"I think I'll write a letter to my mother and tell her I'll be home for Christmas," said Robert Gruebel.

"Good idea." Corporal Kosnar sat down on his bunk and reached for his writing pad. "I think I'll do the same thing."

"I don't have to write home," grinned Sergeant Gallivan. "I'll be there tomorrow night."

"Lucky guy," Kosnar said enviously.

Very little was said until shortly before 1:30 P.M. Then Sergeant Gallivan slipped off his bunk and pulled on his flight jacket. "All right," he called, "it's time to go."

"I'm ready," declared Private Gruebel.

"Kosnar?"

Allen Kosnar was sitting on the edge of his bunk. "I . . . I . . . I'm not going." There was a puzzled look on his face. "You go ahead. I'll see you when you get back." To this day, Allen Kosnar isn't sure just why he suddenly decided not to go out on Flight 19. He had no reason at all to think that something might go wrong.

"Oh, come on, Kosnar," said Gallivan.

"No. No, I'm not going." The corporal shook his head.

"I've been flying too much lately. I . . . I . . . I just don't want to go out today. I don't know why, but I just don't want to."

Gruebel and Gallivan looked at one another. Both of them knew that although it was still early in the month, Kosnar had already put in the required number of flying hours for December. If he didn't want to go out on Flight 19, he didn't have to. Those were the regulations.

"Sure you're not coming, Kosnar?" asked Gallivan.

"Positive. My mind's made up," declared the corporal. "I'm staying here."

Allen Kosnar didn't know it then, but his decision not to go out on Flight 19 that day saved his life.

Gallivan, Gruebel, and eleven other men from Flight 19 sat in the briefing room and fidgeted. It was time to take off, but their flight leader still hadn't shown up.

Lieutenant Charles Taylor, the leader of Flight 19, finally arrived at 1:45 and called the duty officer aside. "Can you find someone to take my place?" he asked. "I don't feel like going out today."

"Why not?" asked the duty officer. "Aren't you feeling well?"

"I feel all right," Taylor told him, "but I just don't want to take this one out. It's as simple as that." This was the only excuse he offered.

The duty officer looked the flight leader over carefully. Taylor was a highly experienced pilot. He had over 2,500 hours of flying time to his credit and most of that time had been spent flying in combat. Unfortunately, he would have to do some more flying today because there was nobody else to take his place. "I'm sorry, Taylor," the duty officer said. "There's no relief available, so I'm afraid Flight 19 is all yours."

"O.K." The flight leader shrugged his shoulders. "If I've got to go, I've got to go."

There were five TBM Avenger torpedo bombers in Flight

Torpedo bombers like the five that disappeared on Flight 19

19. All of them had been carefully checked by aircraft mechanics. The fuel tanks were full, the survival gear was intact, and all instruments were in perfect working condition. The weather was favorable and no problems of any kind were anticipated.

Pilots generally agreed that the Avenger was a fine aircraft to fly. One of the largest and most powerful single-engine planes ever built, it had a 1,600-horsepower engine and flew at nearly 300 miles an hour. It could carry either a torpedo or 2,000 pounds of bombs. The crew consisted of a pilot, a radioman, and a gunner. Gallivan and Gruebel were in an Avenger piloted by Captain George Stivers.

The men in tower control watched lazily as the five planes took off into the clear sky. Captain Edward J. Powers, Jr., a marine student pilot, was in the lead position. Lieutenant Taylor was bringing up the rear. The time was ten minutes past two.

There was nothing at all exciting about Flight 19's mission. It was to practice low-level bombing at a place called Hens and Chickens Shoals near the Bahama Islands. The next step was to continue to fly east for another 67 miles and north for 73. It would then fly west-southwest for 120 miles. That done, the flight would return to the Fort Lauderdale Naval Air Station. Its day's work would be finished.

The afternoon of December 5, 1945, however, was not like any other day for Flight 19. Lieutenant Robert F. Cox, the senior flight instructor at Fort Lauderdale, was getting ready for takeoff at about 3:40 P.M. when his radio crackled. The voice seemed to come from someone on a ship or plane, and that someone was in trouble. The transmissions seemed to be directed to "Powers." The voice asked Powers a number of times what his compass read, and finally Powers said, "I don't know where we are. We must have gotten lost after that last turn."

Cox, now in the air, gave his radio call signal as FT-74. "This is FT-74," he called. "Plane or boat calling 'Powers' please identify yourself so someone can help you."

The voice identified itself as FT-28, the radio call signal for Flight 19. "FT-74, this is FT-28. Both my compasses are out and I am trying to find Fort Lauderdale, Florida. I am over land, but it's broken. I am sure I'm in the Keys but I don't know how far down and I don't know how to get to Fort Lauderdale."

That's strange, thought Lieutenant Cox. He's over the Keys? Both of his compasses are out? Taylor had flown in the area for six months and he ought to know whether or not he was over the Keys. Something must have gone wrong because Taylor's voice was frightened and confused. "What is your present altitude, FT-28?" asked Cox. "I will fly south and meet you."

FT-28 replied, "I know where I am now. I'm at twenty-three hundred feet. Don't come after me."

Don't come after me! The strange words were just too much for Lieutenant Cox. There was something definitely wrong. "I'm coming to meet you," he called.

A few minutes later, there was another call from Flight 19. "This is FT-28. Can you have Miami or someone turn on their radar and pick us up? We don't seem to be getting far. We were out on a navigation hop and on the second leg I thought they were going wrong, so I took over and was flying them back to the right position. We have just passed over a small island. We have no other land in sight. I'm sure that neither of my compasses are working."

Cox was now as confused as Taylor. How could Flight 19 have run out of islands if he was in the Florida Keys? he wondered. And how could he possibly have missed the Florida peninsula? And why didn't Taylor want Cox to come after him? It was all very, very strange indeed.

At 4:26 P.M., Air-Sea Rescue at Fort Everglades heard FT-28. "Does anyone in the area have a radar screen that could pick us up?"

Air-Sea Rescue went into action at once. They had no direction-finding gear, but they asked other stations along the coast to attempt to pick up the lost flight on radar or with direction finders. Over twenty land facilities were asked to try to locate Flight 19. Merchant ships in the area were asked to be on the alert and several Coast Guard vessels were told to be ready to put to sea.

Meanwhile, Lieutenant Cox was having his own problems in keeping contact with the lost flight. "Something is wrong, FT-28. Your transmissions are fading. What is your altitude?"

"I'm at forty-five hundred feet." The reply was very weak and seemed to come from far away.

Cox's transmitter went out at this point. He could no longer keep in contact with the Avengers, but he was sure he knew why the transmission had kept getting weaker. While he had been flying south, the lost flight had been flying north. They had actually flown out of radio contact with one another. Flight 19 wasn't anywhere near the Florida Keys. It was most likely over the Bahamas and Cox was certain that he could find the lost planes.

As soon as he got back to Fort Lauderdale, Cox told his story to operations and requested permission to take another aircraft out to search for the flight. The answer he received was, "Very definitely, no." It was a bitter disappointment for Lieutenant Cox. To this day, he is convinced he knew where the lost flight was, but he was denied the opportunity to prove his point.

The Fort Lauderdale operations officer, however, agreed with Cox. He believed that the planes were lost over the Bahamas and he passed this message on to Air-Sea Rescue. Flight 19 was instructed by Air-Sea Rescue at 4:30 P.M. to fly 270 degrees. At the same time, a pilot in the flight was heard to say, "If we fly 270 degrees, we'll hit land."

There was no indication that this instruction had been received. Apparently it wasn't, because at 4:45 P.M. Taylor announced that "we are heading 030 degrees for 45 minutes, then we will fly north to make sure we are not over the Gulf of Mexico." Eighteen minutes later, however, he radioed to his flight to "change course to 090 degrees for ten minutes."

The other pilots disagreed violently. "No!" one exclaimed. "Head west, damnit! Head west!"

"If we don't fly west, we'll never get home," another protested.

Everyone on shore knew that the situation was desperate. It was now five o'clock. Darkness was coming on fast and the weather was rapidly getting worse. There was a low ceiling over the Bahamas and poor visibility. Lieutenant Taylor was completely lost. He kept asking the other pilots what course they were on and for how long they had been on it. If he continued to fly east and north he would get progressively farther and farther from land.

To make matters even worse, radio communication was very poor. There was a great deal of static and constant interference from Cuban radio stations. Air-Sea Rescue finally called FT-28 and told him to switch to 3000 kilocycles. This was the search and rescue frequency and it would guarantee better reception between the flight leader and the shore facilities. Taylor, however, refused to change over. "I cannot switch frequencies," he called. "I must keep my planes intact." No one could blame him for that decision. If Taylor had switched to a frequency of 3000 kilocycles, he would no longer have been in contact with the other planes.

A search plane was preparing to leave Fort Lauderdale to look for the lost flight when another message came in from FT-28. Taylor radioed that they would fly 270 degrees until they hit the beach or ran out of gas. This was wonderful news. If Flight 19 maintained a bearing of 270 degrees, the planes stood an excellent chance of getting back to land. Once they were close enough to shore, they could be picked up by radar or direction finders and guided to the nearest landing field. Optimism ran so high that the search plane was kept on the ground.

The optimism, unfortunately, didn't last long. At four minutes after six, Taylor was heard calling to his flight. "We didn't go far enough east," he told them. "Turn around again. We may just as well turn around and go east again."

It was a tragic decision. Taylor still believed that he was over the Gulf of Mexico, but the other pilots were convinced that they were over the Atlantic Ocean and that a bearing of 270 degrees would get them home.

Things kept getting worse. Darkness had fallen and a storm was raging. The captain of the British tanker *Viscount Empire* was northeast of the Bahamas at that time and he reported to Air-Sea Rescue at Fort Lauderdale that the ship had encountered tremendous seas and winds of high velocity in the area. Hope for Flight 19 began to fade. Every minute that passed carried it farther and farther from shore.

Weak and garbled messages continued to be picked up from Flight 19. "All planes close up tight . . . will have to ditch unless landfall . . . when the first plane drops to ten gallons, we all go down together."

At about 6:00 P.M., the approximate location of Flight 19 had been determined. The Navy and Coast Guard placed it within a 100-mile radius of 29 degrees north and 79 degrees west. The planes were north of the Bahamas and east of New Smyrna, Florida. If this information could be given to Lieutenant Taylor, he could get home by flying due west.

Taylor never received the information and Flight 19 supposedly continued to fly east. The transmissions became weaker and weaker, then faded out completely at 7:04 P.M. The five Avengers and their crews would have to ditch in the sea. There could be very little doubt about that. They would run out of gas at approximately eight o'clock.

A huge Martin Mariner PBM-5 flying boat took off from the Banana River Naval Air Station at exactly 7:27 P.M. to search for Flight 19. The pilot was Lieutenant Walter G. Jeffrey and there were twelve men in the crew. The plane carried enough fuel for a twelve-hour flight. Three minutes after takeoff, the aircraft radioed an "out" report to its home base.

That was the last word ever heard from the giant flying boat.

It had disappeared as completely as the five planes in Lieutenant Taylor's flight.

By dawn of the next day, the largest air-sea search and rescue mission in history was underway. Two hundred and forty-two planes and eighteen ships were already on the lookout when the sun came up. The aircraft carrier *Solomons* and her thirty-five planes joined the search at noon. More ships and planes arrived later in the day. The British assisted in the search by sending out every available plane at the Royal Air Force Base in the Bahamas.

The search was not confined to the sea alone. Land parties scoured the beaches in the Bahamas and Florida Keys. Men tramped along the Florida coast hoping to find one shred of evidence. Weasels, marsh buggies, and other vehicles groped their way through bleak swamplands. Helicopters and even a Navy blimp flew over the wild, desolate region. There was a faint possibility that Flight 19 may finally have turned west and crashed somewhere on the peninsula. Although this didn't seem very likely, nothing could be left to chance.

The first hint of what may have happened to the big Martin Mariner flying boat came from the tanker S.S. *Gaines Mills*. A message received from the tanker read: "At 1950 [7:50 P.M.], observed a burst of flames, apparently an explosion, leaping flames 100 feet high and burning for ten minutes. Position 28 degrees 59 minutes north, 80 degrees 25 minutes west. Stopped, circled area using searchlights, looking for survivors. None found." Her captain later confirmed that he saw a plane catch fire and immediately crash, exploding upon the sea.

A message received later from the aircraft carrier *Solomons* confirmed the report from the tanker. It stated that "Our air search radar showed a plane after takeoff from Banana River last night proceeding on a course of 045 degrees at exact time S.S. *Gaines Mills* sighted flames and in exact spot the above plane disappeared from the radar screen and never reappeared."

The position given by the *Gaines Mills* was precisely

where the Martin Mariner would have been twenty-three minutes after takeoff. The plane, it seemed, had caught fire and exploded. Airmen referred to the Martin Mariner as "the flying gas tank" because of the huge fuel tanks built into the hull. Gas fumes often filled the planes and smoking was strictly forbidden. It was customary for the pilot to search each crew member for matches and cigarettes before a flight. "Isn't it possible," someone suggested, "that Lieutenant Jeffrey was in such a hurry to find the missing Avengers that he completely forgot to take this precaution?"

Although ships and planes rushed to the scene, neither survivors nor debris were sighted. This was certainly strange. The *Gaines Mills* had been on the scene almost immediately and seen nothing. An explosion would have blown the big plane to bits, so why was nothing found? This is a question that has never been satisfactorily answered.

Another report was received at Air-Sea Rescue headquarters on the third day of the search. Captain J. D. Morrison, an Eastern Airlines pilot, said that he was flying southwest of Melbourne, Florida, at two o'clock in the morning and could see red flares and flashing lights in the middle of a swamp. Although he was unable to see any wreckage, he could see people standing in the light of the flares. A Navy plane was sent out to investigate and the pilot radioed back that he could also see flares.

A small army of men arrived at dawn and the entire area was searched thoroughly. Not a single clue was found, but the searchers learned something that only added to the mystery. Farmers living near Melbourne reported that three nights earlier they had heard a tremendous explosion and seen a huge flash in the sky.

This was the same night that the six planes had disappeared and the same night that the *Gaines Mills* had reported an explosion.

So far, nobody has been able to explain the flashing lights

and red flares seen by Captain Morrison and the Navy pilot.

After five days and five nights of frenzied activity, the ships and planes of the rescue operation were finally called home. Three hundred and eighty thousand square miles of land and sea had been searched thoroughly and not a shred of evidence had been found. Six planes and twenty-seven men had vanished without a trace.

The mystery actually began before the planes even left the ground. Neither Corporal Allen Kosnar nor Lieutenant Charles Taylor wanted to go out on Flight 19. "I can't explain why," Kosnar reported recently, "but for some strange reason I decided not to go out that day." Kosnar was lucky. Taylor, too, wanted to remain in camp, but he was the flight leader and couldn't be replaced. Whether or not it was some form of premonition that told the men not to fly that day is not known.

A Naval Board of Inquiry investigated every aspect of the case. Experts from several fields were called in, but they were as confused as everyone else. After a week of closed sessions, a member of the board issued a statement to the press. He was quoted as saying, "This unprecedented peacetime loss seems to be a total mystery, the strangest ever investigated in the annals of Naval aviation."

Quite a few people were convinced that they knew exactly what had happened to the missing planes and men. Unfortunately, most of their theories were too farfetched to be seriously considered.

An engineer in New York submitted a set of very detailed and complex drawings to the Naval Board of Inquiry. His drawings supposedly proved that there had been a massive midair collision. Somehow or other, the huge flying boat had managed to fly head-on into the five Avengers and all six planes had then plummeted straight down into the sea. The engineer's drawings showed how such a collision *might* have occurred, but they left too many questions unanswered. A collision would have strewn wreckage over a large area, but no debris of any kind was ever found. Among other things, the collision theory also failed to explain how experienced pilots could have gotten lost.

Several letters suggested that the planes had been blown far out to sea by heavy winds. No wreckage or survivors had been found because the planes and ships engaged in the search had not gone far enough out into the Atlantic. This theory was promptly shot to pieces by the Navy who insisted that the winds on the night of December 5 were not strong enough to blow the Avengers off their course.

It was ridiculous to suppose that all of the planes could suddenly have developed serious mechanical difficulties, yet this was suggested in a number of letters. The Navy wouldn't go along with this idea at all. If the planes had ditched, it was because they had run out of gas and not because of any mechanical troubles. But if the planes had ditched, why were there no survivors? "The Avenger crews were so well trained in ditching procedures that they could get onto their life rafts without even getting their feet wet," stated a naval officer.

Not everyone agreed. Some former Avenger pilots thought that a plane ditching at night in a heavy sea would probably not survive the crash. Others declared that out of a flight of five planes there would almost certainly be some survivors.

Naval and Coast Guard officials weren't quite sure what to think about some of the more creative theories put forward. Dr. Manson Valentine, a well-known explorer, said, "The twenty-seven missing men are still here, but in a different dimension as a result of a magnetic phenomenon that could have been set up by a flying saucer."

Equally confusing is the theory advanced by Dr. Stanley Krippner of the Maimonides Medical Center in New York. He believes that a black hole in space called a vortex exists in the area where the planes disappeared. A vortex, he explains, is a place where people do not act as they normally would. They actually become different people and see things in an entirely different way. To put it more simply, a vortex could probably be described as a giant whirlpool that can be found on land, on sea, or in the sky. "Planes and ships that enter a vortex don't come out," says Dr. Krippner.

Literally thousands of people were convinced that flying saucers were responsible for the disappearance of the planes and their crews. They believed that beings from outer space kidnapped Flight 19 and carried it off to another planet for observation purposes. This was one theory that the Navy and the Coast Guard refused to accept. They know that unidentified flying objects have been reported in the area with alarming frequency. The military has fat files on these sightings, yet they maintain a stubborn silence. Flying saucers are something that they steadfastly refuse to discuss. Not Dr. Valentine, however. He says, "It is more than curious that so many incidents happen in this area and that so many UFOs are seen not only in the sky but entering and leaving the ocean."

Many sightings of UFOs are never reported and there's a good reason for this. "A lot of pilots have seen a lot of strange things that they can't explain," a young naval officer said softly. "If they report them or talk about them, though, it damages their reputations. More than one pilot who reported seeing unidentified flying objects has wished that he'd kept his mouth shut."

The officer shrugged his shoulders and made a gesture with both hands. "It's really weird, isn't it?" he went on. "If we report seeing something that we can't explain or understand, they think that we're seeing things that don't exist. Well, a pilot who insists that he's seen something that doesn't exist is going to find himself in trouble, so he simply doesn't report what he's seen."

We have no way of knowing, of course, whether flying saucers had anything to do with the disappearance of the planes and men. We do know, though, that very strange things are going on in the area in which they disappeared—an area that has earned for itself the name of the Devil's Triangle.

The Devil's Triangle

A bulletin put out by the United States Coast Guard in Miami, Florida, states that "the 'Bermuda or Devil's Triangle' is an imaginary area located off the southeastern Atlantic coast of the United States, which is noted for a high incidence of unexplained losses of ships, small boats, and aircraft. The apexes of the triangle are generally accepted to be Bermuda, Miami, Florida, and San Juan, Puerto Rico, but we know of no maps that delineate the boundaries of the Bermuda Triangle."

The boundaries of the Bermuda or Devil's Triangle depend entirely upon who has drawn the map. John Wallace Spencer, who first focused world attention on this area, insists that the triangle must extend as far east as the Azores, which seems to be a logical theory because many ships and planes have disappeared without a trace between the Azores and Bermuda. Also in this part of the Atlantic a number of vessels have been found without a single person aboard. No one has ever been able to discover what happened to the captains, crews, or passengers.

Some authorities believe that the area is incorrectly

named. "It's not a triangle at all," said the late Ivan Sanderson who devoted a lifetime to studying inexplicable phenomena, "it's shaped like a lozenge." British writers insist that it's rhombus-shaped and refer to it as the Rhombus of Death. Richard Winer, the Fort Lauderdale yachtsman who produced a documentary film entitled *The Devil's Triangle*, says that the area is a square. "We can't call it that, though," he states, "because nobody would know what we were talking about."

This is quite true. The names Bermuda Triangle and Devil's Triangle were introduced to the world by author Vincent Gaddis in 1964. Since that time, this area has also been called the Hoodoo Sea, the Triangle of Death, the Jinxed Sea, the Sea of Lost Souls, the Sea of Oblivion, the Limbo of the Lost, the Atlantic's Graveyard, the Triangle of Terror, and a number of other eerie names.

In spite of its evil reputation, this is a strikingly beautiful part of the world. The blue waters are wonderfully clear. Palm trees wave gracefully back and forth on long, sandy beaches. Dolphins frolic merrily around the boats of native fishermen wearing huge, floppy straw hats. Skin-divers laze slowly along over coral reefs of incredible beauty. Warm ocean breezes send yachts skimming easily from island to island. Tourists by the tens of thousands splash around happily in the sea off Miami Beach. They most likely don't know it, but they're splashing around in the Devil's Triangle.

Unfortunately, this region can be as deadly as it is beautiful. Sudden storms seemingly spring up out of nowhere. Howling winds of hurricane force can turn a tourist paradise into a desolate wasteland in a matter of minutes. Freak waves swamp the boats of the most seasoned sailors and even send large ships to the bottom. A yacht driven onto a jagged coral reef stands almost no chance at all. Giant waterspouts shoot up and can knock planes right out of the sky. Many a sailor has come to grief in the swift, turbulent, and extremely dangerous waters of the Gulf Stream.

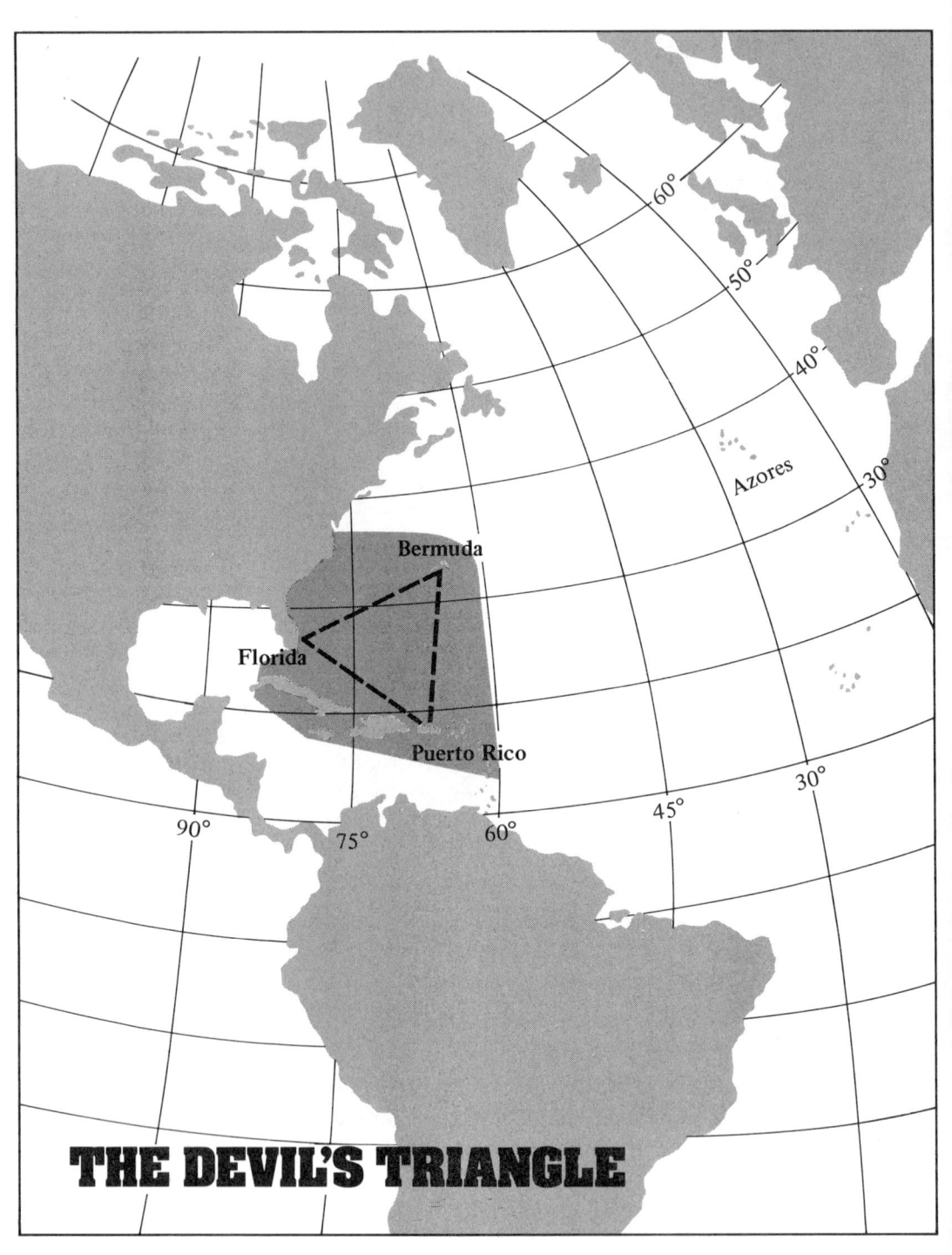

Men in Miami's Seventh Coast Guard District have a very healthy respect for the Devil's Triangle. They freely admit that there have been a great number of mysterious and frightening disappearances that cannot be explained. There are, however, far more disappearances that can be explained quite easily. "Hundreds of pleasure boats travel the waters between Florida's Gold Coast and the Bahamas," said a junior officer. "All too often these crossings are attempted with too small a boat, insufficient knowledge of the area's hazards, and a lack of good seamanship. These guys capsize or get lost and we have to try to find them."

Finding a man lost at sea, I learned, is a mighty hard job. "This woman just called and said that her husband should have been back three days ago," a Coast Guardsman in Miami's district headquarters told me while poring over a map. "He went fishing on Saturday and she hasn't seen him since. She's worried sick, of course, but she waits for three days before calling us." He scratched his head and frowned. "We've had strong winds the last couple of nights and the guy could be just about anywhere. He could be here or here or here," he said, stabbing at his charts. "He might be in a hotel in the Bahamas, he might be out in the Gulf Stream by now, or he might be on the bottom of the Atlantic. We don't know where he is, but we've got to try and find him."

The Coast Guardsman worked in silence for a few moments, then: "We're up against so many things, you see," he continued. "There's an awful lot of ocean out there and trying to find someone in a small boat is sort of like trying to find that needle in the haystack that people are always talking about. It's not easy. We've got to consider the wind velocity, strength of the currents, time elapsed, direction, speed of the guy's boat, and all the rest of it." He paused and dropped his compass onto the chart. "The ships and planes can't start searching, of course, until we tell them where we think the guy might be."

"How long does the search go on?" I asked.

"Five days at the most," I was told. "If we don't find him in that time, we have to give up."

"And that's one more victim for the Devil's Triangle," I said.

"Not really, no. The guy was a victim of his own negligence or inexperience. There's nothing mysterious about a man who disappears at sea because he went out in a boat that was too small." The Coast Guardsman spoke slowly, drumming his fingers on the chart. "The only real victims of the Devil's Triangle are the highly experienced pilots and seamen who vanish mysteriously through no fault of their own. They've taken every precaution, but they disappear without a trace and nobody knows what's happened to them."

An example of this kind of unsolved mystery occurred only a mile from the line of luxury hotels on Miami Beach. It happened in 1967, just a few days before Christmas. Thousands of tourists crowded the resort and everything was gaily decorated for the festive season. It was a lovely sight and two men decided to see how it looked from the sea. They were Dan Burack, a Miami Beach hotel owner, and Father Patrick Horgan, a Catholic priest from Fort Lauderdale.

At nine o'clock that night, the Coast Guard received a radio-telephone distress call from Burack. His cabin cruiser had become disabled, he reported, and he would like a tow back to his hotel marina. The Coast Guard told him to fire a flare in about twenty minutes. The flare could be seen for miles around and would guide the rescue boat to the cabin cruiser.

This was strictly routine stuff for the men at Seventh District Headquarters of the U.S. Coast Guard in Miami. They received an average of twenty-three distress calls a day and this was simply another one. All they had to do was to rush out to the disabled cruiser and tow it to shore.

Something, though, had gone wrong this time. There was no flare to be seen anywhere. Neither was there any sign of the *Witchcraft*, Dan Burack's cabin cruiser. The men in the rescue boat tried to make radio contact with Burack but received no reply.

This was a most peculiar situation indeed. Even if they hadn't seen the flare, they should be able to see the lights of the cabin cruiser, the men in the rescue boat reasoned. They knew, though, that no flare had been fired because they couldn't possibly have missed seeing it. What had gone wrong? they wondered. Why weren't they able to make radio contact with Burack and why didn't he have his lights on? He had radioed headquarters earlier, so his boat must have power.

Although the Coast Guardsmen were confused, they weren't overly alarmed. The *Witchcraft* had to be out there somewhere. Even if she had dragged anchor, she couldn't be far away. Besides, the two men on board her weren't in any real danger. The cabin cruiser had water-tight flotation chambers that made her unsinkable. There were also life jackets and other emergency equipment on board. Then, too, Dan Burack knew every inch of these waters. He was an expert sailor and not the type of man who would panic in an emergency. Neither would he run any foolish risks.

The rescue boat continued to run back and forth parallel to the beach and found nothing. By this time, the Coast Guardsmen were beginning to believe that they had a problem on their hands. Burack would not radio for a tow, then accept help from someone else and not notify headquarters. He couldn't have made it back home under his own power, either, and that meant that he and Father Horgan must still be on board the *Witchcraft*.

A search of the adjacent waters revealed nothing, so a plan of action had to be formed. Sending out a search mission seemed rather ridiculous. They would be trying to find a cabin cruiser and two men who couldn't possibly be missing. There was no other choice, however, and the alert was called in to headquarters in Miami.

A fruitless and frustrating air-sea search followed. The

Coast Guard, the Civil Air Patrol, and private boats and aircraft combed the area from the Florida Keys north to St. Augustine and 120 miles out to sea. Vessels equipped with underwater scanners probed the ship channel and its surroundings. Small craft sailing in the Bahamas and off the Florida coast were asked to be on the lookout for the missing cabin cruiser.

It wasn't until the third day after Christmas that all hope was abandoned. Twenty-four thousand five hundred square miles of ocean had been searched and not a single sign of the *Witchcraft* or the two men on board her had been seen. "We know that the men are missing," someone quoted a Coast Guard spokesman as saying, "but we find it hard to believe that they are lost at sea."

The mysterious disappearance of Dan Burack and Father Patrick Horgan made the newspaper headlines, but no one could say for certain what had happened to them.

Although it cannot be considered an explanation, there is one thing upon which nearly everybody agrees: When last heard from, the missing cabin cruiser was in an area lit by the glow of the Christmas lights on Miami Beach. Unfortunately, that peaceful and beautiful area lies within the perimeters of the deadly Devil's Triangle.

This was but one of the many losses for which neither negligence nor ignorance could be blamed.

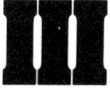

The First Signs of Trouble

As far as is known, the first navigator to record strange happenings in the Devil's Triangle was Christopher Columbus.

About six weeks after leaving Cadiz, Spain, with his three little ships, Columbus sailed into the Sargasso Sea. This is an immense tangle of floating seaweed that covers an area almost the same size as the entire United States.

"Ran into weeds that stretched as far as the eye could see," Columbus wrote in his journal. "The weather and sea were calm and the weeds so dense and matted that the sailors were afraid they couldn't get through. They thought the sea here must be very shallow and they worried about running aground or hitting submerged rocks."

We can't blame the sailors for being afraid. They believed that the vegetation they saw floating in the sea was rockweed. If there was rockweed around, they reasoned, then there must also be rocks. This meant that the sea must be very shallow and they were in danger of running aground at any time.

Columbus understood the fears of his men and tried to calm them. To prove that there was no danger of the ships

A sixteenth-century woodcut showing a whale attacking a ship

hitting submerged rocks, he threw a weighted line over the side. The piece of lead went down deep into the depths, but it never touched the bottom. And we now know why. In most parts of the Sargasso Sea, the ocean is about three miles deep.

Columbus reports that the weather and sea were calm when he sailed into the weeds. This is generally true of the Sargasso Sea. There is very little rainfall, evaporation is high, and the winds are light. The water is warm and remarkably clear.

After the boats had been in the weeds for a week, the wind fell away to nothing. This made the sailors even more unhappy. Whether or not they were aware of the eerie stories told about the Sargasso Sea, we don't know. We can be certain, though, that Columbus knew all about them. The Phoenicians and Carthaginians had dared to venture far out into the Atlantic and they brought some rather wild tales back with them. The stories were so frightening that even experienced sailors were nervous about sailing beyond the Pillars of Hercules—the rocky promontories on either side of the eastern end of the Strait of Gibraltar—into what was the unknown "ocean sea."

The First Signs of Trouble

These early sailors referred to the Atlantic as the Sea of Darkness. The water was shallow and muddy, they reported, and unlucky ships became hopelessly entangled in huge jungles of seaweed. There was no escape. Unless a giant octopus dragged the ship down into the ocean depths, it would stay where it was until it rotted to bits. It was also believed that there wasn't enough air to breathe in this seaweed jungle and entire crews died of suffocation.

On September 15, 1492, Columbus was still in the Sargasso Sea and well inside what is now known as the Devil's Triangle. The sea was calm. A small breeze ruffled the sails and the unhappy sailors wondered whether there would ever be enough wind to blow them back to Spain.

The sun finally disappeared below the western horizon. It became slightly cooler, but the men stayed out on deck. Their sleeping quarters were too hot and cramped for comfort. It was a beautiful night and they couldn't help but admire the majesty of the star-spangled sky.

Suddenly, a loud shout shattered the peaceful quiet of the night. The men leaped to their feet and raced to the rail. A large object of intense brilliance was shooting down from the heavens. None of them had ever seen anything like it. Sailors are usually superstitious and the men on the three small ships were terrified. Fire simply didn't fall out of the sky for no reason at all. It had to be an omen of some kind. A warning, perhaps. A warning from God telling them to leave this strange and frightening ocean and return to the land where they had been born.

Although Columbus couldn't explain what he had seen, the entry in his logbook gives us a clear picture of what happened. "On this night," he recorded, "we were struck with awe at beholding a great flame of fire which fell from the sky into the sea about four or five leagues distant."

So what could this great flame of fire have been? we wonder. It almost certainly wasn't a meteor. Meteors usually burn themselves out of existence many miles above the earth's surface and only very rarely reach the lower atmosphere. A meteor, moreover, would not have been described as a great flame of fire.

Was it a fireball then that Columbus and his men saw? This is a difficult question because scientists themselves regard fireballs as unexplained natural phenomena. They generally agree, though, that fireballs are some kind of illuminated gas or condensed energy that drops from the electromagnetic currents high above us. As these objects enter the earth's atmosphere, they blow up in a blast of furious energy and intense heat. If the fireball seen by Columbus had struck his ships, the story of the discovery of America would have been quite different.

Many hundreds of people have reported seeing fireballs in the Devil's Triangle. Pilots have even told how they had to swerve sharply to avoid being hit by them. It's obvious that a plane could not collide with a fireball and survive the impact.

There are a number of cases on record where people have seen fireballs and at the same time heard a series of explosions in the sky. This could have been what happened on the night of December 5, 1945, the date on which the five TBM Avenger torpedo bombers and the Martin Mariner flying boat disappeared.

UFO, or unidentified flying object, enthusiasts have a theory uniquely their own. They claim that Christopher Columbus was the first white man in the Americas to report a flying saucer sighting. This may or may not be the case. We have no way of knowing whether Columbus saw a fireball, a flying saucer, or something else. The Devil's Triangle was reported as "saucer-ridden" as early as 1952 and reports have been pouring in steadily ever since.

The U.S. Navy Hydrographic Office does not like the words *fireball* or *flying saucer*. They record all sightings of unexplained lights and fires in the sky as "celestial phenomena." "A disproportionately high number of sightings of celestial phenomena occur in the region known as the Devil's or Bermuda Triangle," a spokesman admitted.

Just ten days after seeing a great flame of fire fall from the sky, Columbus and his men had another terrifying experience. They were almost swamped by giant waves that suddenly appeared out of nowhere.

"There all at once came a heavy swell of the sea unaccompanied by any wind," Columbus recorded in his journal. "Great waves pitched the vessels about and the sailors who couldn't understand this phenomenon were more frightened than ever."

It's no wonder that the sailors were frightened. The sea was calm. There wasn't even enough wind to fill the sails, yet they suddenly found themselves being tossed helplessly about by giant waves. This was simply too much for them. Everyone knew there couldn't be waves without wind.

Actually, the mystery of freak waves unaccompanied by even a breath of wind is still not completely understood. However, Dr. Joanne Simpson, a weather expert at the experimental meteorological laboratory located on the University of Miami campus, has solved a part of the mystery. Dr. Simpson believes that the waves are caused by something she calls neutercanes. "Neutercanes are freak storms of great intensity," she says. "They're several miles in diameter and often last only a few seconds. But they stir up giant waves and you have wild seas coming from all directions. These neutercanes," she adds, "can be devastating."

Columbus and his men were lucky. Freak waves well over one hundred feet high have sent an untold number of ships to the bottom. One of the unlucky ones was the *Mormackite*, a large ore freighter. She was sailing alone peacefully on a calm sea in 1954 when suddenly she was struck square on the beam by a monstrous wave. The vessel was flipped over onto its side with such force that eleven men were hurled clear of it. The survivors stared in shocked astonishment as their ship disappeared into the depths. It's fortunate that Columbus and his little fleet didn't suffer the same fate.

Tangled jungles of seaweed, great flames of fire, and freak waves of monumental proportions weren't the only problems Columbus had to face. He had also been having difficulties with his compass. It was acting very peculiarly and he couldn't imagine why.

Columbus couldn't have known, of course, that he had sailed into one of the two areas in the world where the compass needle points to true north rather than magnetic north. This poses no problem for today's navigators. Their charts give them the exact degree of compass variation and they're able to plot their course accordingly. Columbus, however, had no charts at all and had never heard of compass variation.

"The pilot took the star's amplitude and found that the needle had moved a whole point of the compass," he recorded. One point of the compass is eleven and a quarter degrees and this was the variation between the port of Cadiz and his position in the western Atlantic on September 17, 1492. As Columbus sailed west, his compass varied more and more each day because the magnetic North Pole was coming into a direct line between his ships and the true North Pole. Columbus, though, had no way of knowing why the needle had moved and this must have added greatly to his worries. He knew that there was something wrong with the compass, but he didn't know what it was.

The peculiar behavior of the compass was just about the last straw for the men. They were terribly frightened of this strange and unknown sea where so many things happened that they couldn't explain. This was truly the Sea of Darkness, they told one another, and God had set His hand against them. He had sent fire down from the skies as a warning. The giant waves unaccompanied by wind were another warning. And now even the compass was not behaving as it should!

This was the most frightening thing of all. They were

An Indian drawing of Indian rulers surrendering to Spanish conqueror Hernando Cortes—seated and wearing feathers in his hat

hundreds of leagues from home. Unless the compass could be put right, they would never again see the sunny hills of Spain. Columbus, they believed, was leading them to a watery grave in this strange sea that they hated and feared.

The crew became progressively more unhappy and Columbus had to invent a little story to keep them from complete despair. The compass was perfectly all right, he assured them. It had only acted strangely for a time because the star he had used to plot his position had moved slightly to the northwest. He now had the new location of the star and there was nothing to worry about.

The unschooled sailors accepted Columbus's story as the truth and the three ships sailed through the Devil's Triangle and on to greater things.

The discovery of the New World couldn't have happened at a better time. The national treasury of King Ferdinand and Queen Isabella was almost empty. As a result of this discovery, however, immense wealth flowed into their treasury in the next years.

Gold was only one of the many treasures brought back by the Spanish galleons from the New World. Silver, precious stones, spices, cocoa, a rare red dye called cochineal, exotic woods, and Indian slaves were also carried away. Perhaps no other treasure hunters in history reaped as rich a reward as the Spaniards in the New World.

Although ships and crews perished at sea, galleons continued to shuttle back and forth between Spain and the New World. The risks were great, but there was no other way to carry the treasure back home.

It wasn't possible for Spain to keep her good fortune a secret. Other nations heard about the wealth in the Americas and they wanted their fair share. And why not? There seemed to be riches enough for everyone. Ships from Great Britain, France, Holland, Portugal, and Denmark set sail for the New World and the greatest treasure hunt in history was on.

Spain wasn't one bit happy about everyone flocking into what she considered to be her own territory. There were riches left and she didn't want to share them with anyone.

The entire Western world was literally up for grabs. One island after the other was seized by European nations, and settlements appeared along the North, South, and Central American coasts. Privateers and pirates had a heyday and not a single settlement dared stop worrying about being attacked.

But the privateers and pirates had their problems, too. They soon learned that these clear blue waters were treacherous in the extreme. Shoals, reefs, hurricanes, and sudden violent squalls struck terror into the heart of even the most dauntless sailor. Tales of shipwrecks were heard constantly. Tales of ships that had simply disappeared were commonplace. The sinister reputation of the Devil's Triangle was rapidly coming into its own.

The Disappearance of Theodosia Alston

Neither Christopher Columbus's navigational problems nor the disappearance of countless galleons raised any suspicions about the Devil's Triangle. Communications were virtually nonexistent—and the trip to the New World was considered so hazardous that a large percentage of the ships weren't expected to return anyway.

It wasn't until nineteenth-century America that a disappearance story captured the public imagination and caused general theorizing about what could have happened in the area now known as the Devil's Triangle.

The story involved one of the most beautiful women in early American history. Theodosia Alston was the young wife of the governor of South Carolina. Her father was Aaron Burr, a former vice-president of the United States.

Tragedy was very much a part of Theodosia's life. She was still a child when her mother died. Although she loved her father dearly and hated to leave him, she married Joseph Alston and moved to South Carolina. Theodosia was only seventeen at the time.

A baby was born during her second year in South Carolina and Theodosia named him Aaron Burr Alston. She worshiped her son and her husband. Only the fact that she was so far away from her father kept her from being perfectly happy.

Then her snug little world began to fall apart. In the summer of 1804, word reached South Carolina that her father had fought a duel with Alexander Hamilton, a brilliant statesman who had been a member of the First Continental Congress. Hamilton had been fatally wounded in the duel and a warrant was issued for Burr's arrest. The charge was murder in the first degree.

The former vice-president of the United States went into hiding. Although he didn't appear at his trial, the court found him not guilty of murder and treason. Burr, however, felt that he was no longer safe in America. He had made many enemies and he felt that he had to get out of the country for a time. With a heavy heart, he packed his bags and sailed for England in 1808.

After four years Burr returned to New York and Theodosia was overjoyed. Aaron Burr Alston was a lovely child and she wanted him to see his grandfather. Theodosia eagerly made plans for the long trip to New York, but tragedy again struck the beautiful young First Lady of South Carolina. Shortly before sailing, her little son contracted malarial fever and died in her arms.

Theodosia's grief was almost more than she could bear. She had loved her son with all her heart and now he was lost to her forever. In her anguish, she blamed everything on the climate of South Carolina. How could anyone be healthy in such heat and humidity? she kept asking. Theodosia was a New Yorker and no one in New York had ever contracted the deadly malarial fever.

Governor Joseph Alston watched his wife with growing concern. She was still remarkably beautiful, but her terrible grief was affecting her health. It would be best for her to have a complete rest and change of scenery, he decided. A few months away from South Carolina might do her a lot of good.

Her father was now in New York and perhaps a visit with him would help to restore her health.

Getting to New York, however, presented certain difficulties. Traveling overland was out of the question. Theodosia simply wasn't strong enough to make the long, uncomfortable trip by coach. She'd have to go by sea. But that also presented problems. The country was at war with Britain, whose ships lurked off the Atlantic Coast ready to attack any unwary American vessel that dared to leave port. New York Harbor had been blockaded by the British, and American ships could neither enter nor leave.

Governor Alston's problems were solved by an unexpected visitor. Timothy Green, Aaron Burr's close friend, arrived in Charleston shortly after Christmas. The former vice-president had sent him to South Carolina to escort his daughter back to New York. All of the arrangements had already been made. She would sail from Georgetown on a ship called the *Patriot.*

Compared to modern-day hostilities, the War of 1812 was a rather genteel affair. When Aaron Burr requested safe passage for the *Patriot*, the British readily consented. They knew that the First Lady of South Carolina would be on board and they promised to do what they could to speed the *Patriot* on her way.

Theodosia, her maid, her personal physician, and Timothy Green left the governor's mansion early on the morning of December 30, 1812, for the fifty-seven mile journey to the port. There were tears in Joseph Alston's eyes when he kissed his beautiful wife good-bye.

He couldn't have known it at the time, but he would never see her again.

Aaron Burr had chosen his ship and captain with great care. The *Patriot* was a speedy little packet that had been built for carrying mail, passengers, and freight from one port to another. Since the outbreak of war with England, she had been turned into a privateer and preyed busily on British shipping. Now, though, her guns had been dismounted and stored below deck. They wouldn't be needed because the enemy had granted the *Patriot* safe passage.

Captain William Overstocks, master of the *Patriot*, was an able and highly experienced officer. He had spent many long years sailing the Atlantic coast and few men knew it better. The trip to New York should have been an easy run. If the weather remained fair, they would have made port in five days.

The little ship weighed anchor soon after Theodosia Alston and her party came on board. Although it was the last day of the year, the weather was surprisingly mild. A moderate wind filled the sails and the *Patriot* sailed bravely out into the Atlantic.

It was never seen again.

Newspapers had a field day. Everyone wanted to know what had happened to the beautiful woman who was the First Lady of South Carolina and the daughter of a former vice-president of the United States. Readers refused to let the story die. They clamored constantly for more details. Every known incident in Theodosia's life appeared in the papers and every reader recognized her photograph instantly.

It's only natural that the British were accused of foul play. They were the enemy and their promise of a safe passage meant nothing. It was, in fact, no more than a cheap and dirty trick. Knowing that the *Patriot* would be sailing from Georgetown, British men-of-war had lain in wait outside the harbor. As soon as the defenseless ship had come in range, they had blasted her to bits.

America was at war with Britain, it's true, but this idea couldn't be further from the truth. Actually, the disappearance of the *Patriot* was an acute embarrassment to the British. They knew that some people would point an accusing finger at them and these suspicions were understandable. After all, anything can happen in a war, but honor must still be maintained. Englishmen would not grant safe passage to a ship, then blow her out of the water. This just wasn't done.

The British actually did everything in their power to find out what had happened to the *Patriot* and her distinguished passenger. The captain of every ship between Georgetown and New York was questioned and the answers were always the same: Nobody had seen a thing. The *Patriot* had not been captured or sunk by the enemy. The British were in no way responsible for the disappearance of the little ship.

Years passed, but the story of Theodosia Alston was not forgotten. It's always big news when a beautiful and famous woman disappears under mysterious circumstances. Editors have to keep their readers interested and everyone likes a mystery.

Nearly a quarter of a century after the *Patriot* sailed from Georgetown, the name of Theodosia again made the front pages of newspapers throughout the country. An old man lay alone and sick in a cheap hotel room in Mobile, Alabama. He kept shouting out in his delirium and a doctor was called. After the patient had calmed down somewhat, he told the doctor an incredible story.

The old man said that he had once served on a pirate ship. They had attacked and boarded a packet called the *Patriot*. One of the passengers was a rich and well-known lady by the name of Theodosia Alston. The lady and all the other captives were forced to walk the plank.

And now the lady had come back to haunt him. No matter where he looked, there she was. As he lay dying, he could again hear her begging for mercy. But there had been no mercy. Like the others, she had walked the plank to her death. The old man knew that she was dead, yet he also knew that she was right there with him in the shabby hotel room.

There was nothing the doctor could do. The former pirate had confessed his sins and would soon be dead.

Other confessions from other former pirates followed in rather short order. A Frenchman named Jean Baptiste Callistre claimed that he had been a gunner on the *Vengeance* when she captured the *Patriot*. Everyone on board the packet had been executed with the exception of a very beautiful woman. The lady was carried over to the *Vengeance* to keep the crew amused. The ordeal was too much for her. She died on Galveston Island in the Gulf of Mexico and was buried near the old fort.

There were more confessions by former pirates and a number of reports from people who claimed that they had inside information. The most recent accounts appeared in a South Carolina newspaper in 1963—a century and a half after the tragic affair.

Theodosia had kept a detailed record of the voyage, the writer reported. The record showed that the *Patriot* had run into terrible storms. Alarmed by the ferocity of the winds, Captain Overstocks turned his little ship around and headed south. Several days later, they sailed calmly into the warm waters of the Bahamas. There was nothing to worry about now, Captain Overstocks assured his passengers.

But Captain Overstocks was wrong. He and Theodosia were both up very early the next morning. Except for the seaman at the wheel, they were the only ones on deck. It was a beautiful day and Theodosia stood beside the captain. A ship was approaching in the distance and he was studying it through his telescope.

Suddenly, he gave a little start. The ship was flying the skull and crossbones. They were about to be attacked by pirates!

Theodosia wasted no time. Dashing down to her cabin, she hastily added a few sentences to her record of the voyage. She then put the notes into a bottle, shoved the cork in firmly, and tossed it overboard. A hundred and fifty-one years later, the bottle was found on a lonely beach in South Carolina.

Whether any of these stories are true or not is something we will most likely never know. It's possible, of course, that the *Patriot* was captured by pirates. It's also quite possible that Captain Overstocks steered his little ship south to get out of the path of a storm.

If that should be the case, then Theodosia Burr Alston, First Lady of South Carolina and daughter of a former vice-president of the United States, disappeared in the Devil's Triangle.

The Saga of the *Mary Celeste*

Whenever people talk about mysteries at sea, someone is certain to mention the *Mary Celeste*. More has been written about this unlucky little vessel than about any other ship that has ever sailed the seas. Today her bones lie rotting off Port-au-Prince, Haiti, in the Devil's Triangle. But, strangely enough, the circumstances of her death are no mystery. The *Mary Celeste* was deliberately driven onto a reef by her captain.

Bad luck hounded the ship from the very beginning. She was launched at Spencer Island shipyard, Nova Scotia, in 1861 and originally named *Amazon*. Her first captain died before he had a chance to take her to sea. A new captain was given command and he immediately managed to damage her hull in a collision with a fishing boat. The following year, she ran into a brigantine off the coast of France and sent it to the bottom.

In 1867, only six years after being commissioned, the ill-starred *Amazon* ran aground on Cape Breton Island. Her owners thought that she was too badly wrecked to bother with, but a man by the name of Alexander McBean thought differently. McBean bought the ship, pulled her back into the sea, and fixed her up as well as he could. That done, he sold her to a New York shipping firm who changed her name to *Mary Celeste*.

The *Mary Celeste*, the shipping firm soon discovered, was no bargain. Dry rot was destroying her timbers and the entire bottom had to be replaced. It was an expensive business, but the owners had no choice. There was no point in owning a ship that wasn't seaworthy.

By the fall of 1872, the *Mary Celeste* was in excellent condition. She was towed to a pier on New York's East River and loaded with 1,701 casks of commercial alcohol. The cargo was to be taken to Genoa, Italy. It was that trip across the Atlantic that was to make the *Mary Celeste* the most famous mystery ship in history.

Benjamin Spooner Briggs, captain of the *Mary Celeste*, came from New England Puritan stock. Although he was only thirty-seven years old, he was a tough and experienced sailor. He read the Bible daily and most of the books in his cabin were of a religious nature. He was a good man who had the full respect of the entire crew.

Captain Briggs was also a devoted family man. He didn't like the long absences from home and had decided to take his wife and two-year-old daughter with him on the long voyage to Genoa. His son had to be left with relatives. He was eight years old and couldn't be taken out of school.

Two nights before sailing, Captain Briggs had dinner with his friend Captain David Reed Morehouse. Captain Morehouse was the master of the *Dei Gratia*. His ship was tied up alongside the *Mary Celeste*. He also had a cargo for Europe, but wouldn't be sailing for another eight days.

On the morning of November 7, 1872, the *Mary Celeste* proceeded slowly out to sea. Strong winds were blowing, but there was no cause for alarm. The ship was in good shape and the crew was reliable. Captain Briggs, in fact, was looking forward to a pleasant and uneventful voyage. His wife's piano had been brought on board and they could spend some of the long evenings singing hymns and reading the Bible.

On November 15, Captain David Morehouse steered the *Dei Gratia* out into the Atlantic and set a course for Gibraltar. The voyage from New York to the Azores was strictly routine. Heavy seas could be expected at that time of the year, but they made normal progress.

The Azores were behind them when the crew of the *Dei Gratia* spotted a brigantine in the distance. The ship seemed to be in trouble. Some of her sails were missing; others were badly torn and fluttering by the corners. Captain Morehouse studied the ship through his telescope, then ordered the mate to steer toward her.

There was definitely something wrong with the brigantine, Captain Morehouse concluded. She was moving slowly and didn't seem to be holding a course. Even more strange was the fact that there didn't appear to be anyone on deck.

The sea was running high and it took nearly two hours to bring the *Dei Gratia* within hailing distance. Captain Morehouse put the megaphone to his mouth and called out over the sounds of the Atlantic. There was no reply. The slap of the waves against his ship was all he could hear. They were close enough by now, however, for him to read the name on the stern.

The mystery vessel was the *Mary Celeste.*

Captain Morehouse was utterly amazed. What had happened to her? he wondered. And where was his friend Briggs? He had left New York on November 7 and it was now December 4. By this time, he should have arrived in Genoa. Something must have happened somewhere at sea. But what? The ship was obviously in trouble, yet she wasn't even flying a distress signal.

As soon as the brigantines were alongside, First Mate Oliver Deveau and two seamen lowered a boat and rowed over to the drifting vessel. They examined the ship thoroughly and everything seemed to be in order.

There was one thing, though, that they simply couldn't understand. Not a single soul, living or dead, was to be found anywhere on the *Mary Celeste.*

A painting showing the crew of the *Dei Gratia* finding the *Mary Celeste*

What happened to the people on board the *Mary Celeste*? This is a question that has been asked tens of thousands of times, but the answer will never be known. The mystery of the *Mary Celeste* is the most famous puzzle of the sea.

The last entry in the logbook had been made on November 25 and there was no hint of trouble. The brigantine was then between Bermuda and the Azores. Whatever it was that happened must have happened on that day. After the disappearance of everyone on board, the *Mary Celeste* sailed on alone until she was spotted by the *Dei Gratia* nine days later.

It's impossible to believe that everyone was swept overboard by heavy seas, as some people have suggested. Captain Briggs would never have permitted his wife and baby daughter to come out on deck in bad weather. There is also reason to believe that they left the ship in a small boat. Evidence pointed to the fact that there had been a boat on board and that it had been launched. There was no way of knowing, of course, whether everyone had left in it.

First Mate Deveau reported that the *Mary Celeste* appeared to have been abandoned very quickly. So quickly, it seemed, that those on board had even neglected to take food and drinking water with them. Captain Briggs had left his raincoat and boots in his cabin. The crew had left almost everything behind. Deveau declared that they had not taken their pipes and tobacco and this was certainly an indication of great haste or panic. It looked as though a small boat had been lowered into the sea and everyone had abandoned ship.

But what was the reason for it? Why had the *Mary Celeste* been abandoned? She was in no danger of sinking or breaking up, so why was everyone in such a hurry to get off her? Captain Benjamin Briggs was a man who knew the sea well. Only the most serious emergency could force him to leave his ship. Unless he thought she was doomed, he would never put his wife and baby daughter into a small boat far out in the stormy Atlantic.

It's a rule of the sea that the captain's first concern must be the safety of his passengers and crew. That would be doubly true in this case. The captain's wife and daughter were aboard and he would certainly consider their safety first.

Another rule of the sea says that the captain must stay with his ship as long as there is even the faintest hope of saving her. Some seamen even believe that it's a captain's duty to go down with his ship if she can't be saved, and many a captain has done just that. Benjamin Briggs had an added interest in bringing his ship safely home. He had bought one third of the *Mary Celeste* and the purchase had taken all of his life's savings.

First Mate Deveau of the *Dei Gratia* could easily see that the *Mary Celeste* had been abandoned in a great hurry, but he couldn't imagine why. He suspected, however, that there had been panic on board. It looked as though the small boat had been lowered hurriedly, and that everyone had immediately climbed in and begun rowing at a furious rate.

This made no sense at all. The sails of the *Mary Celeste* were still set. Captain Briggs was an experienced seaman. He knew that only a small breeze would be enough to blow the *Mary Celeste* away from them. Men rowing a small boat would never be able to catch up with her. A man with his wits about him wouldn't have dreamed of doing such a thing. He would have tied a rope to the stern of the ship and let the boat be towed along behind. In that way, he could easily have gotten back on board once the danger had passed.

Although Oliver Deveau examined the ship from stem to stern, he could find nothing wrong with her. Her cargo was intact, there was plenty of drinking water and enough food to last for six months. Once the sails had been repaired, the *Mary Celeste* would be seaworthy enough to be sailed around the world.

Deveau returned to the *Dei Gratia* and made his report to Captain Morehouse. He suggested that the *Mary Celeste* be sailed to Gibraltar where they could claim salvage. This meant that the shipping company would pay them the value of the ship and her cargo. Captain Morehouse agreed. They had found a rich prize and the extra money would come in handy.

Unfortunately, their reception in Gibraltar was far from a warm one. Some officials were convinced that the crew of the *Dei Gratia* had murdered everyone on board the *Mary Celeste*, then seized the ship and cargo.

Mr. Solly Flood, the Queen's Attorney of Gibraltar, was a most difficult and peculiar little man. He decided that there had been foul play on board the *Mary Celeste* and nothing could make him change his mind. Everyone on the *Mary Celeste* had disappeared; therefore, the crew of the *Dei Gratia* must be guilty of foul play.

As far as Mr. Flood was concerned, there was no mystery at all. Captain Benjamin Briggs, he argued, certainly wouldn't abandon his ship in the middle of the Atlantic. The cargo alone was worth over $30,000. Besides, why would he suddenly leave a seaworthy vessel and take off in a small boat with his wife, baby daughter, and crew? This was an absolutely ridiculous idea! No, maintained Mr. Flood, there could only be one answer: Captain Morehouse and his men had committed murder and piracy on the high seas.

There were others who were inclined to agree with the Queen's Attorney and perhaps they shouldn't be blamed. After all, it was most unusual to find a seaworthy ship floating along with nobody on board. People just didn't step off ships in the middle of the Atlantic, so it was quite clear what had happened: They had been murdered and thrown off.

When the court examined the *Mary Celeste*, Mr. Solly Flood found evidence of violence and foul play wherever he looked. There were marks on the rail that had been made by an ax and others that had been made by a sword, he insisted. Then a sword was found under Captain Briggs's berth. There were tiny brown stains on it and Mr. Flood declared positively that blood had caused the stains. Similar stains were found on the deck and these, too, were said to be blood.

Now foul play really did come into the picture. A doctor who analyzed the stains submitted a report stating that it was not blood that was found on the deck and the sword. This bit of evidence was not to Mr. Flood's liking. He kept the doctor's report a secret and even refused to let the United States Consul see it. Meanwhile, he kept insisting that Captain Morehouse and First Mate Deveau confess whose blood had been spilled. He also insisted that they explain the marks on the rail.

Poor Morehouse and Deveau were having a bad time of

it. A charge of murder and piracy was hanging over their heads. Neither one could explain the marks on the rail or the blood stains because they knew nothing about them. They could only tell what had actually taken place, but that wasn't good enough for the Queen's Attorney. He simply refused to believe their story.

The suspicious mind of Mr. Solly Flood was never idle. He told the court that the *Mary Celeste* could not possibly have sailed along by herself for nine days. If that had been the case, she would have been found hundreds of miles farther south. The fact that the last entry in the logbook had been made on November 25 meant only one thing: The crew of the *Dei Gratia* had boarded the *Mary Celeste* on that day and simply neglected to keep the logbook up to date. Unfortunately, there was no way to disprove this.

During the hearings, one of the owners of the *Mary Celeste* informed the court that Captain Morehouse sometimes used an alias. Solly Flood, of course, made the most of this. Only a treacherous and unprincipled man would use a name not his own, he loudly declared. If a man had nothing to hide, then why would he use another name? He must be trying to hide a criminal past or something equally sinister. It's not known why Morehouse used an alias, but this fact only added to the suspicion that already hung over him.

The most idiotic thing that the Queen's Attorney produced before the court was a letter written to him by the sister of Albert Richardson, the *Mary Celeste*'s first mate. The story of the trial on Gibraltar was big news in all the world's papers and she had, of course, followed it closely. After giving the matter a great deal of thought, she had come to the conclusion that the crew of the *Dei Gratia* was responsible for her brother's death and she had stated her suspicions in the letter.

Although the letter meant nothing whatsoever, Mr. Solly Flood waved it about triumphantly. Here, he declared, was further proof of murder and piracy.

This latest act of lunacy must have amazed members of

the court. Suspicion was not evidence. The fact that Richardson's sister believed that the crew of the *Dei Gratia* was guilty was of absolutely no importance. She had seen none of the evidence. She hadn't heard any of the testimony. And she had never met Captain Morehouse, First Mate Deveau, or any seamen from the *Dei Gratia*. She merely believed them to be guilty and had written a letter saying so. Anyone else could have done the same thing.

The hearings on Gibraltar lasted for three long months. By the end of that time, the court was thoroughly fed up with the antics of the Queen's Attorney. He was determined to convict the crew of the *Dei Gratia* and would let nothing stand in his way. He had even suppressed evidence in his vain effort to get a verdict of guilty.

Captain Morehouse and his crew sailed from Gibraltar in March 1873. They had been found not guilty by the court, but Mr. Flood managed to get in one last cruel blow. The *Dei Gratia* should have been awarded approximately $45,000 for bringing the *Mary Celeste* into port. In a final gesture of defiance, Solly Flood reduced this amount to a mere $8,500.

Shortly after the *Dei Gratia* left Gibraltar, the *Mary Celeste* was returned to her owners. Captain George Blanchford arrived in Gibraltar from New York and sailed her to Genoa, where he unloaded her cargo.

The *Mary Celeste*, the most famous mystery ship in history, was then sailed back to the United States.

Over a century has passed since the *Mary Celeste* was found sailing the Atlantic without a single soul on board. In spite of all the time that has gone by, the mysterious events surrounding her are still as fascinating today as when they happened.

Nearly every maritime museum in Europe and the Americas has a model of the ship. Nobody can even guess how many newspaper features, magazine articles, and books have been written on the subject. The Atlantic Mutual Insurance

Company in New York, which insured the brigantine, has an entire room devoted to material written about her. The *Mary Celeste* Museum is in the same building.

What happened to the people on board is a question that has been asked many thousands of times. Some theories are worth considering; others are extremely far-fetched.

It's perhaps safe to say that the crew of the *Dei Gratia* was in no way responsible for whatever it was that took place on the decks of the *Mary Celeste*. We can also be quite sure that everyone was not swept into the sea by a giant wave. The theory that a giant octopus jerked the people off one by one can also be dismissed. So can the theory that everyone suddenly caught a dread disease and jumped into the storm-tossed Atlantic to end their suffering.

Some flying saucer enthusiasts maintain that Captain and Mrs. Briggs, their daughter, and the crew were spirited away into space by an unidentified flying object. This is an exciting theory, but it doesn't hold up. The boat on board was missing and there would be no need for a boat in outer space.

As so often happens, old seamen in ports from Hong Kong to Hamburg claimed to have been on the *Mary Celeste*. Their days at sea were over. They had only death to look forward to, but they wanted their names to live on after them. They told wild stories of mutiny, piracy, and a captain gone berserk. Although the stories were interesting, they were soon proved to be false.

In the more thoughtful versions of what took place on board the ship, Captain Briggs usually emerges as the culprit. Some people believe that he went mad and murdered his wife, daughter, and the crew. When he regained his senses and realized what he had done, he threw himself overboard in a fit of remorse. Heavy seas breaking over the ship would most likely have washed away any blood stains.

A much less bloodthirsty theory is that a barrel of alcohol exploded in the hold. Afraid that the entire ship was going to blow up, Captain Briggs hurried everyone into the boat and rowed away to safety. Deveau reported that those on board seemed to have left in great haste. Briggs, himself, left so fast that he didn't even take the time to make one final entry in the logbook. If he had done that, the disappearance of those on board the *Mary Celeste* would never have been a mystery. Those who support this theory make a point of the fact that Captain Briggs panicked and behaved like a coward. His concern for the safety of his wife and daughter is understandable. Why, though, did he abandon a ship that was still sound?

Another version also puts the blame on Captain Briggs. The last entry in the logbook states that the ship was then within six miles of Santa Maria Island. The sea was calm. There was no breeze to fill the sails, but a steady current carried the brigantine closer and closer to the shore. Something had to be done quickly or the *Mary Celeste* would be pounded to bits on the rocks.

The boat was lowered. The crew helped Mrs. Briggs and her daughter get settled in the stern, then climbed in after them. Captain Briggs followed. Two seamen grabbed the oars and began rowing away from the dangerous line of rocks. A stiff breeze suddenly came up and filled the sails of the *Mary Celeste*. The people in the small boat watched in helpless misery as the ship sailed away toward the open sea.

Poor Captain Briggs must have been the most miserable of them all. He should have stayed with his ship for as long as there was the faintest glimmer of hope, but he had abandoned her. Now he had lost his ship, and the lives of his wife, daughter, and crew were in the most terrible danger. A short moment of panic and cowardice had cost him everything he loved in life.

When Captain George Blanchford tried to hire a crew to sail the *Mary Celeste* to Genoa to unload her cargo of alcohol, he found himself with a difficult problem: Sailors are a superstitious lot and none of them wanted to sail on an ill-starred ship. The *Mary Celeste* meant bad luck and they wanted no part of her.

The evil reputation of the *Mary Celeste* lived on. Misfortune had plagued her on her first voyage and it continued to hound her wherever she went. Nobody wanted to know the unhappy little ship. Seamen considered her a jinx. Captains were reluctant to take her out to sea. Owners were certain that she brought them bad luck and they soon tried to get rid of her. In the last twelve years of her life, the *Mary Celeste* was owned by the incredible total of seventeen different firms.

On December 16, 1884, the *Mary Celeste* left Boston for Port-au-Prince, Haiti. She was twenty-three years old and she looked it. Barnacles covered her bottom. She leaked badly in heavy weather and her hull was scarred. Paint hung from her in strips and her sails were far from new. There was nothing at all beautiful about her.

Captain Gilman Parker, master of the *Mary Celeste*, was at the wheel when the ship entered Haiti's Gulf of Gonave on January 3, 1885. The captain knew that a coral reef called Rochelois Bank lay in the southern channel and he steered straight toward it. Just before reaching the reef, he ordered an inexperienced seaman to take the wheel and keep to their present course.

This was the most cruel trick imaginable. The young sailor saw the reef almost as soon as he took over. He made a furious effort to turn the ship, but it was too late! With a sickening crunch, the *Mary Celeste* smashed into the jagged coral. Water poured into the hold and Captain Parker ordered the crew to bring the cargo onto the deck. There was no danger of the ship breaking up. She was perched solidly on the reef and the weather was fine.

After spending the night on the stricken vessel, the crew rowed ashore. Captain Parker's first act was to sell the cargo.

The Saga of the Mary Celeste

Although it was insured for $30,000, he sold it to the United States Consul on Haiti for a paltry $500. As soon as the cargo had been removed from the ship, the captain poured kerosene over the deck and set her on fire.

The ill-starred *Mary Celeste*, a mystery ship that still excites the interest of millions, had made her last voyage.

It's probably not surprising that the curse of this unfortunate little vessel did not die with her. An insurance agent in Boston studied the case and became suspicious. He was convinced that both the ship and her cargo had been insured for far more money than their actual value. An investigator was sent to Haiti and he made some startling discoveries.

The cargo, he learned, was not even worth the $500 that the United States Consul had paid for it. Barrels marked ale were full of water. Sixty-four cases of boots and shoes turned out to be shoddy rubbers. A heavily insured case listed as cutting instruments contained dog collars. Many barrels, crates, and cases contained nothing at all.

But that was only the beginning. It was perfectly obvious that Captain Gilman Parker had deliberately wrecked the *Mary Celeste* on Rochelois Bank. The deliberate destruction of a vessel is called barratry and was punishable by death under the laws of the United States.

Captain Parker and three members of the shipping firm that had supplied the worthless cargo were put under arrest. Parker was charged with barratry and conspiracy to defraud. The other three men were only charged with conspiracy to defraud.

The jury was unable to come to a decision. It was obvious that they sympathized with Parker. The captain was sixty-one years old at the time of the trial, but humiliation, fear, and the weight of his sins made him appear much older. It seemed heartless to condemn a desperately unhappy old man to certain death. The jury asked the judge if it would be possible to find Parker innocent and the others guilty, but the judge ruled that this could not be done.

An order for a new trial was posted and Captain Parker and the other three defendants were allowed to return to their homes. Within days, one of the defendants went violently insane and another committed suicide. The shipping firm for which they had worked was forced to declare bankruptcy. Captain Gilman Parker fell sick and died before the new trial was called into session.

The *Mary Celeste* had been driven to her death in the blue waters of the Devil's Triangle, but her jinx lived on.

Joshua Slocum—
an Unlikely Victim

On May 28, 1967, when Francis Chichester sailed the *Gipsy Moth* into Plymouth Harbor, he was hailed by many as the first man to circumnavigate the world single-handed in a small sailing vessel. A brave and tough old man had conquered the mightiest and most dangerous seas on earth and the world had a new hero.

Absolutely nothing can be taken away from Sir Francis Chichester. His voyage was a truly heroic and monumental achievement. He deserved every bit of the praise that was lavished upon him. Very few people knew, though, that another man had made a solo voyage around the world sixty-nine years earlier. That man was an American named Joshua Slocum.

Joshua Slocum was born on Briar's Island, Nova Scotia, in 1844. The sea was a part of the islanders' lives. They loved it, feared it, and above all had a healthy respect for it. The ships built on Briar's Island were as sturdy as the men who built them and they sailed all the world's seas.

The waters off the coast of Nova Scotia can be terribly

treacherous. Winds called northeasters come howling in straight from the Arctic icecaps. Giant rollers and breakers crash against the rocks with a mighty roar. Fickle currents suddenly change direction for no reason at all. The highest tides on earth foam and froth against shores so hostile that almost nothing can grow there.

Briar's Island may not be beautiful, but it's a fine training ground for future sailors. Shipbuilding and fishing are the chief industries; the sea is the island's livelihood. Boys on Briar's Island know the sea and ships so well that many of them become captains while they are still young men.

The formal education of little Joshua Slocum came to an early end. His father had inherited a rundown farm and left the sea to work it. At the age of eight, the boy was taken out of school and put to work on the farm. The elder Slocum seemed to think that if his son had not received enough schooling by that time, then there was no hope for him. Joshua, however, did a fine job of educating himself. He dearly loved books and never stopped studying.

Shortly after the boy's twelfth birthday, his father caught him making a ship model when he should have been working in the fields. Joshua was given a sound beating and watched in helpless rage as the model of his little ship was smashed. This was too much for him. After gathering together his few possessions, he ran away from home.

Joshua's first job was as cook on a fishing schooner. It was a job he didn't hold for very long since he knew nothing at all about cooking. When the crew looked at the meal he had prepared for them, they chased him off the ship.

At the age of sixteen, Joshua sailed before the mast on a voyage from New Brunswick, Canada, to Ireland. His next trip was on a British ship sailing from England to China. He fell sick in what was then the Dutch East Indies. While in the hospital, he became friendly with a British ship captain who was en route to Australia and planned to return to England by way of various ports in the South Pacific and Far East. When the ship left the Indies, Slocum was on board her. Although he was only eighteen, he sailed as second mate.

After making two trips around Cape Horn in British ships, he went salmon fishing in Alaska. He then hunted sea otters for their skins, but he missed the excitement of the long sea voyages. In 1869, just a few months after his twenty-fifth birthday, he was offered a job as captain on a schooner plying between San Francisco and Seattle.

A year later, he was given command of a ship carrying a general cargo to Australia. After unloading the cargo, he was to take on board enough material to build two fishing boats. Salmon fishing was a profitable business and Captain Slocum's orders were to build the boats in Alaska and bring back all the fish that they could catch.

While the cargo was being loaded in Sydney, Captain Slocum took time off to get married. His new wife sailed with him on the long voyage from Australia at the bottom of the world to Alaska at the top of the world. Although the trip was relatively uneventful, disaster struck while the ship lay at anchor in an Alaskan bay. A violent storm came up suddenly and the vessel was carried high onto the beach. Slocum studied the situation and knew that the vessel could never be refloated.

A lesser man would have forgotten about the fishing, but Slocum hardly batted an eye. The men made tents from the sails and built a fishery. Indians were hired to help the crew and everyone went to work. While the men were out after salmon, Slocum built a thirty-five-foot whaler to carry them all back to civilization.

The season was highly successful. The salted salmon were sealed in barrels and hidden in the forest. All they had to do now was to make their way to Kodiak, the nearest port. It was a tricky and a highly dangerous business, but they arrived safely after a hair-raising voyage. A schooner was sent to bring back the barrels of fish, then everyone returned to San Francisco.

The owners weren't happy when they were told about the loss of their ship. They were pleased with their young captain, however, and gave him another vessel. This time, he would be trading between San Francisco, Australia, and the romantic islands of the South Seas.

Although Slocum had been born in Canada, he became an American citizen and proudly sailed his ships under the Stars and Stripes. Mrs. Slocum usually sailed with her husband and all four of their children were born either on board ship or in foreign countries.

Just about everything that could possibly happen to a sailor happened to Joshua Slocum during his many long years at sea. He ran into pirates, buccaneers, and hostile natives. On two occasions, cholera and smallpox killed off most of his crew. Cyclones and hurricanes smashed several of his ships. Once mutiny broke out while his ship was off the coast of South America. Slocum was forced to kill two men to save his own life and the lives of his wife and younger son.

One of Captain Slocum's greatest seafaring adventures began off the South American coast. A savage storm drove Slocum's schooner onto the rocks. No lives were lost, but there was no hope of saving the ship. The crew took off immediately for the nearest port and Slocum was left on a desolate beach with his wife and two sons. Home was thousands of miles away and they had almost no money.

It was the sort of challenge that Captain Slocum seems to have enjoyed. After calmly discussing the situation with his family, he set to work building a sailing canoe. They were over 5,000 miles from home, but that didn't discourage them.

Six months after the loss of his ship, the Slocum family launched their thirty-five-foot canoe, called the *Liberdade*. Winds and waves buffeted her. Coral reefs tried to rip out her bottom. A giant whale threatened to smash her to bits, but the *Liberdade* sailed bravely on.

On December 27, 1888, a gentle south wind helped the

canoe into the harbor at Washington, D.C. The Slocum family was given a hero's welcome. They had sailed the trusty *Liberdade* for 5,510 miles. Much of that had been over angry seas, but they had made it safely home at last.

The American people honored the brave little *Liberdade* by putting her on display in the Smithsonian Institution where all the world can see her.

Although adventure had always been a part of Joshua Slocum's life, he still dreamed of the greatest adventure of them all. Even as a boy he had talked about sailing alone around the world in a small boat. It had never been done, of course, but Slocum was absolutely convinced that he could do it. The fact that most people considered such a voyage an impossibility only made him more determined.

His big chance came one wintry day in 1892. He was discussing his dream with an old friend in Boston. The man listened in silence, then told Slocum that he would give him a ship if he really wanted to sail alone around the world. The vessel needed some repairs, he added, but it would be very nice once he got it all fixed up.

Early the next morning, Slocum went out to Fairhaven to examine the ship that had been given to him. When he saw it, he roared with laughter. The vessel was an ancient sloop that had been propped up in a pasture over a mile from the sea. His old friend was having a joke at his expense, but Slocum was the kind of man who loved a joke.

Some farmers came along while Slocum was looking at his gift and told him that the ship had been built at the same time as Noah's ark. The captain chuckled appreciatively. The boat was old, it's true, and it needed a great deal of work. His practiced eye, however, told him that the ancient vessel could still be made seaworthy.

"What do you want her for, Captain?" asked one of the farmers.

"I'm going to fix her up and sail her around the world," replied Slocum, his eyes twinkling.

The farmers didn't laugh. They knew that if the famous Captain Joshua Slocum said that he was going to fix the old ship up and sail her around the world, then he was going to do exactly that.

It took thirteen months of hard work to make the *Spray* seaworthy, but it was worth the time and effort. She was a staunch little vessel and Captain Slocum was proud of her. Although she was only thirty-six feet nine inches long, he was sure that she could survive the most savage seas.

The *Spray* sailed from Boston on April 24, 1895. Less than an hour after setting out, Slocum saw a large steamship that had been wrecked. She was the *Venetian*. A storm had driven her onto a rocky ledge and she had broken in half.

It was a sobering sight. The great ship had been powered by steam. She carried a full crew and had the most modern equipment. A pilot had been on board to guide her safely into the harbor, yet she now lay smashed in two on the rocks.

Slocum sailed sadly past the stricken ship. The seas of the world lay before him and he was all alone. He was the captain, crew, and pilot. Only the wind could help him on his way. He didn't have any modern equipment to make his job easier.

His chronometer, an instrument for measuring time with extreme accuracy so that the exact course and position may be plotted, was a battered alarm clock. It didn't have a minute hand, so he had been able to buy it for a dollar. Experienced mariners felt that they couldn't get along without a chronometer, but Slocum had to be content with his old clock. It was all he could afford.

Captain Joshua Slocum's single-handed voyage around the world is one of the greatest stories in sailing history. Only a man with great courage, tremendous stamina, and an iron will could have succeeded. He outraced pirates off the coast of Morocco in North Africa. Hostile Indians attempted to board the *Spray* while it was anchored in Tierra del Fuego at the southern tip of South America and Slocum beat them off. Mountainous seas and howling winds almost swamped him in the treacherous waters of the Straits of Magellan. He was becalmed for a week in the Sargasso Sea. Hurricanes and other tropical storms very nearly sent Slocum and the *Spray* to the bottom on a number of occasions. The endless days of danger and loneliness became an anguished torture, but he refused to give up. He had said that he was going to sail around the world and he was determined to do it. And he did! It took him three years and 46,000 miles of sailing, and the voyage made him a legend in his own day. The name of Captain Joshua Slocum was known to everyone who admired courage and high adventure.

Being a world hero, however, didn't really appeal to Captain Slocum. He much preferred the solitude of the sea to life on shore. The endless round of banquets, interviews, and public-speaking engagements bored him. To escape all this, he sailed the *Spray* down to Grand Cayman in the West Indies every winter. It was warm and peaceful there on the old pirate hideaway and he loved it.

In the early fall of 1909, Slocum again set out for the West Indies in his faithful *Spray*. His lectures and books had earned him a fair amount of money and his boat was well-provisioned. Even after her many years at sea, the *Spray* was still in good condition. Slocum had a decent chronometer now and all of his charts were up to date.

The *Spray*, too, had an added new look. She carried a lantern that lit up her sails at night. The lantern had been a gift from Slocum's friends in Boston. It threw off so much light that nobody could possibly help but see the little ship sailing along in the darkness. Getting run down at night by a larger vessel is something that every yachtsman fears. Now, however, Captain Slocum had no worry on that score.

But it wasn't long before people began worrying about Captain Slocum. The *Spray* was overdue in Grand Cayman. It had been sighted off the Bahamas, then not seen again.

Old sea captains in Boston shook their heads. Where was Slocum? they asked one another. What could have happened to him? He was the master of all sailors and the *Spray* was a stout ship. What could have gone wrong?

It seemed highly unlikely that a man as skillful as Joshua Slocum could have run into trouble. This was his fourth trip to Grand Cayman. He knew those waters well and reports said that the weather had been good. He couldn't have been blown off course. Neither could he have been driven onto a coral reef or ledge of rocks. A steamer hadn't sunk him because the lantern given him as a gift could be seen from many miles away.

Days passed and then weeks. There was no sign of Slocum. Neither was there any sign of the *Spray*. Every vessel in or near the area kept a sharp lookout, but not one of them was able to report a single thing. The brave little *Spray* and her gallant captain had vanished completely.

The old sea captains in Boston discussed the disappearance in low voices. All of them had sailed their ships through those waters. And all of them had heard stories about ships that sailed into that area and were never heard from again. They had simply vanished without trace and no one ever knew why. There was never any debris and never any survivors. The losses were listed as unsolved mysteries of the sea and that was it.

It seemed ironic that the name of the most famous sailor of his time should now be added to the list of unsolved mysteries. Captain Slocum had spent fifty of his sixty-five years at sea. He had been the first man to sail around the world alone. He had faced every danger that a sailor could possibly face and had always come out on top. His courage and determination had been an inspiration to millions.

The world may never know what mysterious force triggered the disappearance of Captain Joshua Slocum on a peaceful voyage to an island he loved. We can be certain, though, that he met that mysterious force with the same bravery he had always shown.

The Suspicious Case of the *Cyclops*

There is no way of knowing how many ships have disappeared without a trace in the Devil's Triangle. Before the days of radio, the public simply wasn't aware of what was happening. Shipping firms and insurance brokers were often the only ones who knew that a ship had disappeared.

Some sailors realized that an unusually high number of ships were vanishing mysteriously in this part of the Atlantic, but this was the sort of thing that they discussed only with other sailors. It wasn't until the U.S.S. *Cyclops* disappeared in 1918 that government officials began to suspect that there was something very strange going on off our Atlantic coast.

The *Cyclops* may have been the last word in marine construction, but she certainly wasn't a pretty ship. Her deck was a maze of booms for loading coal. Her bridge appeared to be too far forward and her twin tunnels too far astern. The overall length was almost the same as two football fields laid end to end. Her weight was just over 19,000 tons; her cruising speed was fifteen knots.

On January 8, 1918, the *Cyclops* was assigned to the Naval Overseas Transportation Service. She was taking on a cargo of coal at Norfolk, Virginia, when the new assignment came through. America was at war and the coal was for U.S. warships serving off the coast of Brazil. It was to be unloaded at the port of Bahia. The big ship was then to proceed to Rio de Janeiro for a cargo of manganese ore. Manganese was vitally important to the war effort and the valuable ore was to be carried from Rio de Janeiro directly to Baltimore, Maryland.

As soon as the cargo had been taken on board, the *Cyclops* headed out to sea. The voyage was anything but a pleasure cruise. It began with a near-collision while the ship was still in Norfolk harbor. It ended with the complete disappearance of the ship in the Devil's Triangle. The *Cyclops* may be dead and buried, but the story of her strange last voyage will never die.

Not a great deal is known about the voyage to Bahia and Rio de Janeiro. Witnesses reported the fact that the *Cyclops* had almost collided with the U.S.S. *Survey*. Officers who had sailed with Lieutenant Commander George W. Worley, captain of the *Cyclops*, accused him of being a poor navigator and other incidents bear this out. Soon after leaving Norfolk, the executive officer and Captain Worley argued over a navigational problem. Worley solved the problem by placing the executive officer under arrest. Most likely the unfortunate man was still in the brig when the *Cyclops* disappeared.

Two other examples of Worley's poor seamanship were received from Brazil. He scraped his ship against a cruiser while drawing alongside to transfer coal. Not a great deal of harm was done, but all damage to naval vessels had to be reported to command headquarters.

The next incident must have staggered his superior officers. Somehow or another, Captain Worley managed to sail his ship right past Rio de Janeiro in the darkness. When daylight came, he found that the *Cyclops* was heading straight for a rocky shore. Only by reversing his engines at top speed was he able to avoid the loss of his vessel.

In spite of the problems and mishaps, Captain Worley

The *Cyclops*

carried on with his mission. His orders were to proceed nonstop to Baltimore. The war was raging fiercely and the manganese was urgently needed for making munitions.

When the *Cyclops* left Rio de Janeiro on February 21, 1918, she was carrying 10,800 tons of manganese ore and 309 men. One of the men was Alfred Gottschalk, the United States Consul General to Brazil. There were also five military prisoners on board. Two of them were marine deserters. The other three were Navy seamen who had murdered a shipmate on the U.S.S. *Pittsburgh*.

For reasons unknown, Captain Worley ignored his order

to sail directly to Baltimore. Instead, he sailed into the harbor of Bridgetown, Barbados, in the West Indies on March 3. This was a most unusual thing to do. The ship could easily reach Baltimore with the fuel and supplies that had been put on board in Rio. Time was extremely important and the stop in Barbados was unnecessary.

Brockholst Livingston, the United States Consul at Barbados, paid an official visit to the *Cyclops* while she was tied up at the pier in Bridgetown. He suspected at once that everything was not as it should be. The executive officer was still under arrest. Several members of the crew had also been arrested because Captain Worley was convinced that they had been conspiring against him with the military prisoners. There was even a rumor that one of the conspirators had been hanged. This was never proved, but the consul included it in a cable to the State Department.

The consul's suspicions must have increased greatly when the *Cyclops* left Bridgetown the following afternoon. Instead of heading north toward the United States, she steamed away to the south. Why? Was a gun being held to Captain Worley's head or was he deliberately steering his ship in the opposite direction of his destination?

These are questions that have never been answered. The *Cyclops* sailed away from the West Indian island of Barbados and disappeared into the unknown.

The Navy was both puzzled and alarmed when the *Cyclops* failed to reach Baltimore. Almost two weeks went by, however, before officials were willing to admit that she was missing. Then swift and intensive action was taken. The secretary of the Navy ordered an all-out search and the big hunt began.

Radio calls from every possible point were beamed to the *Cyclops.* Ships crisscrossed every mile of every route she might possibly have used. Beaches and coves on hundreds of islands were searched for wreckage or survivors. Nothing

The Suspicious Case of the *Cyclops*

was found, but a high-ranking officer told the press that "hope is still felt by the Navy. We refuse to give up the search until every possibility of finding some trace of the ship has been exhausted."

At a press conference a few days later, a spokesman said, "No well-founded reason can be given to explain the *Cyclops* being overdue. We refuse to believe that the collier could have been wiped out without leaving a trace."

But even the hopes of the Navy finally began to fade. "The search still continues," an official press release stated, "but the Navy feels extremely anxious as to the safety of the *Cyclops* and her 309 passengers and crew."

In spite of the war raging in Europe, the loss of the *Cyclops* was headlined in hundreds of newspapers. How could a big ship like that disappear into thin air? people wanted to know. Such things simply didn't happen. When a ship went down, things always broke free and bobbed to the surface. Often, too, there was an oil slick that spread out for many miles. A passing ship couldn't help but notice the huge patch of discoloration floating on the sea.

The question of survivors posed another thorny problem. There were 309 men on board the *Cyclops*. Why, then, were there no survivors? A number of them would certainly have been on deck at all times. Couldn't they have launched a lifeboat? Or even clung to a piece of wreckage? After all, some sailors had survived for several days in just that way.

Another troubling question was the absence of a distress call. Why hadn't the ship sent out an SOS? It would only have taken a few seconds and someone would surely have heard her. For that matter, why had the *Cyclops* maintained radio silence? Nothing had been heard from her since the afternoon of March 4 when she steamed out of Bridgetown harbor. There was no way of knowing whether Captain Worley had turned his ship north or continued to sail south.

A number of people felt certain that the search for the *Cyclops* was a waste of time and money. They were convinced that something very strange was going on in this part of the ocean. The complete disappearance of so many ships was more than a mere coincidence. It was true, of course, that a great number of them had come to grief because of human error and violent storms. Others had been captured and sunk by pirates, buccaneers, and privateers. Those that sailed away and vanished without a trace were simply listed as lost at sea.

This, they felt, had been the fate of the *Cyclops*. She had been lost at sea. She had vanished completely and there was no sense in looking for her. This wasn't really much of an explanation, but it was the only one they had to offer.

Theories as to what happened to the *Cyclops* were a dime a dozen. Perhaps the most interesting one appeared in the *Literary Digest*, an influential magazine of that time. The article was written in all seriousness and it's safe to assume that many people believed it.

The writer suggested that the *Cyclops* might have been sunk by an octopus. While sailing serenely along through the West Indies, the giant creature had suddenly appeared alongside the ship. Tentacles the size of a tree trunk had shot out and wrapped themselves tightly around the hull. The octopus had then dragged the 19,000-ton vessel down into the depths of the Atlantic.

Other theories were less far-fetched, but none of them was ever proved. Some believed that the ship had turned over and sunk after being struck by a freak wave or waterspout. The possibility that one of the boilers had exploded and knocked out the radio so that no distress calls could be made was also considered. So was mutiny on board. It was known that Captain Worley had been having trouble with a certain bad element on the *Cyclops*. Could these men have murdered the captain and anyone loyal to him, then escaped in the ship's boats?

Maybe, but it hardly seems possible. Neither does any of the other theories.

Many favored the belief that the *Cyclops* had been sunk by the Germans. America was at war with Germany and the ship carried a valuable cargo of manganese ore. Brazilian cities like Rio de Janeiro and Bahia were literally crawling with spies. Any of them could have informed the Germans that a ship loaded with manganese was en route from Rio to Baltimore.

This theory could not be discarded until the war was over. A study of the German naval archives then showed that there were no mines, U-boats, or warships in or near the Devil's Triangle at the time of the disappearance of the *Cyclops.*

Although there was never any proof of his guilt, many accusing fingers were aimed at Captain George W. Worley. Investigators learned that his real name was Johann Friedrich Georg Wichmann. He had been born in Germany and had deserted from a German freighter in New York at the age of fifteen. Before the war, his closest friends were German merchant marine officers.

People can hardly be blamed for suspecting Worley. American boys were being killed every day by the Germans and hatred toward Germany ran high. Worley had become an American citizen. He had also worked his way up to lieutenant commander in the United States Naval Reserve Force. This wasn't good enough for many people, though. As far as they were concerned, Worley was still a German and his sympathies were with Germany.

Newspapers carried sensational stories about the captain of the *Cyclops.* Investigators showed that he was an eccentric tyrant who ruled his ship with an iron fist. His favorite punishment was to order the sailors to walk barefoot across the blazing heat of the steel decks. Even his officers were placed under arrest for the slightest offense.

Captain Worley must have been a most peculiar person. Men who had sailed with him reported that he would usually appear on deck wearing long underwear and a bowler hat and carrying a cane. Both officers and crew disliked him intensely.

Except for his wife and his German friends, nobody seems to have had a kind word for him.

Because Worley had been born in Germany and because he had associated with German merchant marine officers, newspapers suggested that he may have surrendered his ship and cargo to the Germans. This accusation brought a howl of wrath from Mrs. Worley. She insisted that her husband was a loyal American citizen who hated Germany. He had served America long and faithfully and would never betray her.

It seems that Mrs. Worley was right. Records in the German admiralty made no mention of the *Cyclops* and no one in the admiralty had ever heard of Lieutenant Commander George W. Worley. No one had ever heard of Johann Friedrich Georg Wichmann either.

On June 14, 1918, the secretary of the Navy ordered the file on the U.S.S. *Cyclops* to be closed. The 309 men who had been aboard her were officially declared dead.

In a final statement, a naval spokesman said, "The disappearance of this ship has been one of the most baffling mysteries in the annals of the Navy. All attempts to locate her have proved unsuccessful. Many theories have been advanced, but none that satisfactorily accounts for her disappearance. All supposed clues to her loss have failed of confirmation."

After a 540-foot ship and 309 men had vanished completely, government officials began to look at the Devil's Triangle with an uneasy eye.

And they've been doing so ever since.

The *Cyclops* had been in service for eight years before she disappeared in the Devil's Triangle. She had proved to be a good ship. Her speed was fifteen knots and she was ideal for carrying large cargoes over long distances. This was the sort of ship the Navy liked and, therefore, a contract was awarded to a Philadelphia shipbuilding firm to build two more just like her. The *Cyclops*'s sister ships were christened *Nereus* and *Proteus* and they were launched in 1913.

For the next twenty-seven years, the two sisters sailed

The *Nereus*

busily from port to port with their cargoes. Both of them seem to have had remarkably unexciting careers. Things in the shipping world, however, were changing rapidly. Faster and larger ships were needed by the Navy. The sisters had done their job well, but their day was over. In 1940, the faithful old vessels were sold to a private company.

Their new job was a routine shuttle service. The *Nereus* and *Proteus* were used for carrying bauxite from St. Thomas in the Virgin Islands to the United States. It was a short easy trip and they usually made two each month.

All went along smoothly until the winter of 1941. Then everything suddenly went wrong. The *Proteus* left St. Thomas for Norfolk, Virginia, on November 23. On December 10, the *Nereus* also sailed from the Virgin Islands for Norfolk. Nei-

The *Proteus*

ther one of the two ships ever reached its destination. Both of them had disappeared without a trace in the Devil's Triangle.

This was a truly incredible situation! How could three ships from the same "family" vanish in the same area? It just didn't seem possible. As far as anyone could tell, the story was the same in every case: No indication of any trouble. No distress calls. No wreckage and no survivors. The big ships had simply ceased to exist.

Compared to the loss of the *Cyclops*, the loss of the *Nereus* and *Proteus* received very little attention. The Japanese bombed Pearl Harbor on December 7, 1941. America immediately declared war on Japan and Germany and this was the news that filled the papers and crackled from radios. The war was uppermost in the minds of all Americans. The loss of

The Suspicious Case of the *Cyclops* 71

two rather strange-looking ships carrying cargoes of bauxite didn't really seem very important at the time.

In spite of the fact that America was at war, ships and planes searched the area thoroughly. Although they knew approximately which course the captains would have set for Norfolk, they found absolutely nothing. The *Nereus* and *Proteus* had vanished as completely as their sister ship, the *Cyclops*.

Many people, of course, blamed the loss of the *Nereus* and *Proteus* on the Germans. We were again at war with them and their submarines and warships were lurking off the Atlantic coast. The two cargo ships could have been picked off as easily as sitting ducks. They carried no guns and were absolutely defenseless.

The war ended in 1945. American officials examined the German naval records, but there was no mention of the two missing ships. At the time of their disappearance, the enemy was watching the major shipping lanes farther to the north.

Officials could come to only one conclusion: Both the *Nereus* and *Proteus* had been swallowed up by the Devil's Triangle. They were listed as lost at sea because nobody knew what had happened to them.

There is an interesting afterword to the story of the *Cyclops*. In the late spring of 1968, the nuclear submarine *Scorpion* left the Mediterranean and headed for her home base in Norfolk, Virginia. There were ten officers and eighty-nine enlisted men on board. The radio officer contacted Norfolk on May 21 and made a routine report. The *Scorpion* was off the Azores and all was well. They would be home within a week.

A week passed, but not another word was heard from the ultramodern submarine. Radio operators working around the clock failed to get any sort of reply. At the end of the second week, the Navy put out an official bulletin saying that the *Scorpion* was overdue and that a search would begin at once.

The nuclear submarine was finally located at the end of October. She was lying in over 10,000 feet of water approximately 400 miles southwest of the Azores. Although thousands of photographs were taken of the sunken hull, the Naval Board of Inquiry failed to find a single clue as to what had happened. "We can only say that yet another chapter has been added to the mysteries of the sea," a spokesman told the press.

It was during the search for the *Scorpion* that a very unusual incident took place. Dean Hawes, a Navy diver from Norfolk, Virginia, was on board the salvage vessel *Kittiwake* when the wreckage of a sunken ship was picked up on the sonar. Hawes went down to investigate and landed on the deck of the strangest ship he had ever seen. "It was a weird-looking thing," he told the author. "About a city block long or maybe longer. There were a lot of upright beams amidships and the captain's bridge was supported by stilts."

The Navy accepted Hawes's report as strictly routine. A search was being carried out for a lost submarine and nobody was interested in an old wreck. Nobody, that is, except Hawes himself. The memory of his strange discovery haunted him, but he had no idea what sort of ship it was that he had found.

It wasn't until Dean Hawes had retired from the United States Navy that he finally stumbled across a clue. He was paging through a magazine when he saw a photograph of the *Cyclops* and the story of her mysterious disappearance in the Devil's Triangle. The former diver sat and stared. The ship in the photo looked very much like the old wreck he had landed on while searching for the nuclear submarine. The resemblance was so great, in fact, that Hawes was convinced that he had actually stood on the deck of the long-lost *Cyclops*.

Having spent twenty-eight years in the Navy, Hawes had of course heard dozens of stories about the strange disappearances of ships and planes in the Devil's Triangle. Now, he thought, there might be a chance that at least a part of the

Dean Hawes, a retired Navy diver, is convinced that he landed on the deck of the *Cyclops* while his salvage ship was searching for the nuclear submarine *Scorpion*.

mystery could be solved. If the Navy could find out what had happened to the *Cyclops*, it might then be able to learn what had happened to other ships that had disappeared mysteriously in the same area.

However, Hawes ran into problems right from the beginning. The Navy's attitude was one of complete indifference. Officers listened politely, then shrugged their shoulders. The former diver had an interesting story to tell, but no one was willing to set any wheels in motion. It was better to forget the whole thing, they implied. The Devil's Triangle was not officially recognized by the Navy. The *Cyclops* had been declared missing in 1918 and it was better to let her stay that way. Moreover, Hawes couldn't prove that the ship he had found was really the *Cyclops*. He may have been convinced in his own mind that it was, but the Navy had to have definite proof.

Although the Navy's lack of interest was a keen disappointment, Hawes refused to give up. He believed that he was in a position whereby he might be able to help solve one of the world's most baffling mysteries and he wasn't going to take no for an answer. There was simply too much at stake.

Hawes's next step was a bold one. The men in the middle weren't willing to help him, so he decided to go straight to the top. He contacted his congressman, Representative William T. Whitehurst of Virginia, and told him his story. Whitehurst promptly arranged an interview with the secretary of the Navy and Hawes hurried to Washington.

The interview was a great success. The Navy's top man was impressed by the former diver's sincerity and common sense. He knew that Hawes had nothing to gain by his persistence. He was only interested in helping to solve a mystery that had always intrigued him. The secretary of the Navy was anxious to solve the mystery because many American ships, planes, and lives had been lost in the Devil's Triangle. As a result of the interview, the secretary directed Captain L. H. Bibby, Assistant Chief of Staff Operations at the Norfolk Naval Base, to plan a search for the strange ship Dean Hawes had landed on.

Captain Bibby was delighted with the assignment. "I hope it really is the *Cyclops*," he told reporters. "I'd love to see one of the biggest mysteries in naval history solved through the efforts of an ex-Navy man."

Although the order for the search had come directly from the secretary of the Navy, a year passed before the search actually got underway. When the U.S.S. *Opportune* steamed out of Norfolk harbor in the late summer of 1974, Dean Hawes was on board as a guest. He had spent a lot of his own time and money trying to get the Navy to investigate the weird-looking wreck he had found and now his dream had come true. As a reward for his persistence, he had been given the right to make another dive down to the ship that had haunted him for so long. It was strictly against the rules for a retired diver to dive from a naval vessel, but the Navy waived the rule and Hawes got into his diving gear.

The diver soon found a sunken hull in 200 feet of water. He knew at once, however, that it was not the same ship he had seen in 1968. "This one was completely different," he wrote in a letter to the author. "The superstructure was different and the angle that it lay on the bottom was different. There is just no way in the world that it was the same ship. Somebody made a mistake somewhere along the line and I dived on the wrong wreck."

Dean Hawes was bitterly disappointed. He is still convinced that he landed on the *Cyclops* in 1968, but the Navy may not make another attempt to find it.

So the fate of the ill-starred *Cyclops* and the 309 men on board her remains as big a mystery as ever.

VIII

The *Carroll A. Deering*

The dawn of January 31, 1921, broke slowly. It was going to be another cold and stormy day. The watchman at the Cape Hatteras Coast Guard Station off the coast of North Carolina shivered as he walked his lonely patrol. Suddenly he stopped and rubbed his eyes! A large schooner had sailed straight up onto the Diamond Shoals. She was still under full sail. Her name was the *Carroll A. Deering*.

Men who hurried over to the stricken ship could hardly believe what they were seeing. They knew that only a madman would carry so much sail in such stormy weather. Something must be terribly wrong. The vessel could certainly have been saved if the sails had been trimmed or lowered. So why hadn't that been done? they asked themselves.

It was four days before the men finally managed to get on board. There was no sign of life anywhere. There were pots on the stove containing soup, meat, and vegetables. The ship had obviously been abandoned shortly before an evening meal. But why? There was nothing wrong with the vessel. The fact that she was carrying full sail indicated that the captain and crew had left during relatively calm weather. Unless, of

The *Carroll A. Deering*

course, she was carrying full sail because someone *wanted* her to be wrecked.

None of it made any sense. Why would the men abandon ship if there were no danger? It was the middle of winter. Furious storms frequently lashed the Atlantic and men in small boats would have very little chance of survival. They would stay on board as long as there was the faintest glimmer of hope. The only thing that could drive them into the lifeboats would be either force or complete panic.

There appeared to be no signs of panic, however. Someone had taken the ship's papers, clock, logbook, and chronometer. The crew had apparently had enough time to take some extra clothing with them. Most of the captain's possessions were no longer in his cabin. One thing, however, seemed very strange: A large, heavy trunk was missing. It hardly seemed likely that he would have taken such a bulky object into a small boat.

A closer investigation of Captain Willis B. Wormwell's cabin brought some interesting and confusing facts to light. There were *three* pairs of rubber boots in a closet. All three were of a different size and must have belonged to different men. Someone had also been sleeping in the captain's spare room. There was no sign that a woman had been on board, so it couldn't have been his wife. Although Captain Wormwell never drank, there were several bottles of rum in the cupboard and there were indications that some heavy drinking had been taking place.

A chart left on the schooner told a strange story. The captain had marked the course in pencil until January 23. Then it appeared that someone else had taken over because the writing changed. Whoever that someone may have been, he continued to mark the course until the ship was abandoned somewhere between Cape Lookout and Cape Hatteras.

This meant that Captain Wormwell had not been in command of his ship for the last seven days. Something had surely gone wrong. Had he died or had he fallen sick and been taken below decks? Had he lost his life in the storm or had he been murdered? His body was nowhere on board, so he had either left in one of the boats or his body had been thrown into the sea. In the latter case, his large trunk would most likely have been thrown in after him.

After the story of the *Carroll A. Deering* appeared in the press, some more facts were revealed. In a letter to his brother-in-law, the captain had confided his worries about the voyage. Something told him that he had very little time left on earth. While his cargo was being unloaded in Rio de Janeiro, he said almost the same thing to another captain. He was having difficulties with his crew, he declared, and his first mate, Charles McLellan, was a worthless and incompetent troublemaker. It was a very worrying situation.

There were more problems when the ship arrived in Barbados. Captain Wormwell told the ship's agents that it was almost impossible for him to control his unruly men. Besides, he himself was in poor health. He was sixty-six years old and would retire at the end of the voyage. Almost all of his life had been spent at sea. The time had now come for him to settle down and enjoy his remaining years.

The crew of the *Carroll A. Deering* ran completely wild in Bridgetown, Barbados. Charles McLellan, the first mate, was picked up for drunken and disorderly conduct and thrown in jail. While there, he loudly boasted to the other prisoners that he would pitch the captain over the side before the ship reached Norfolk. In spite of McLellan's evil and dangerous character, Captain Wormwell got him out of jail so that he could leave on the schooner. He also managed to get the rest of the crew sober enough to go back to work.

On January 9, 1921, the *Carroll A. Deering* left Bridgetown harbor. Her course to Norfolk, Virginia, would take her north through the Devil's Triangle. This was exactly the same course that the ill-starred *Cyclops* had taken just three years before.

The *Carroll A. Deering* lost both her anchors in mountainous seas two days before she was driven aground. This fact was established when she passed the *Cape Lookout* lightship on the afternoon of January 29. The incident was reported by Captain Thomas Jacobson at a later date.

The ship came by with all sails set. She was riding the water like a giant swan and looked so beautiful that the captain took a photograph of her. Although there was no real indication of trouble, Captain Jacobson suspected that something strange was going on aboard.

His suspicions were soon confirmed. The men were standing together on the quarter-deck in an idle group. This was a lack of discipline that no captain would have permitted. As a matter of fact, the captain was nowhere in sight. A man with red hair and a foreign accent hailed the lightship with a megaphone. He said that the *Deering* had lost both anchors in a storm and asked that this be reported to Norfolk.

Captain Jacobson wasn't sure what to think. It was normally the captain who passed on such messages and it was the custom for him to identify himself to the captain of the lightship. The man with the red hair was certainly not the schooner's captain. He didn't even look like an officer.

So where was the captain of the *Carroll A. Deering*? Jacobson wondered. If he were sick or dead, why hadn't it been reported? The loss of a skipper was much more important than the loss of the anchors.

The account submitted by Captain Jacobson confused the investigators even more. They suspected by now that Captain Wormwell had not been in command of his ship when it passed *Cape Lookout*. They had no idea, though, what had happened to him. There was no way of knowing whether he was dead or alive.

The man with the red hair and foreign accent couldn't be explained either. There had been no man answering to that description on board the schooner when she sailed from Barbados. So who was he? And how had he gotten onto the

Deering? Why was he the one who had reported the loss of the anchors? If the captain was sick or dead, why hadn't one of the other officers made the report?

Piracy seemed like a wild idea, yet it also seemed to be a possible answer. Pirates could have boarded the ship and murdered the officers. The crew may have been standing idly on the quarter-deck when the *Deering* passed the lightship because someone was holding a gun on them.

The suggestion that it may have been piracy suddenly received support. A man with the unusual name of Christopher Columbus Gray appeared with a bottle that he had found on a beach in North Carolina. A message inside said that the *Deering* had been captured by another ship. The crew had been handcuffed and there was no escape. The message asked the finder of the bottle to notify the owners of the *Deering*.

This was piracy on the high seas and the Departments of State, Commerce, Justice, and the Treasury now joined the Navy and Coast Guard in the investigation. All of these agencies had been concerned about the large number of ships disappearing off the Atlantic Coast. They finally had a clue and they followed it up quickly.

Handwriting experts declared positively that the note had been written by Henry Bates, the *Deering*'s engineer. If Bates had been in the engine room at the time of the attack by the pirates, he would probably have had enough time to write the message and throw it into the sea.

Shortly after Christopher Columbus Gray turned his bottle over to the authorities, another bottle was picked up by a British liner. A message found inside had supposedly been written by Willis B. Wormwell. It declared that he had been taken prisoner by his crew and had been placed aboard another vessel.

Now confusion really did set in. Mrs. Wormwell studied the message and insisted that it had not been written by her husband. The note in the second bottle was passed off as a cruel hoax, but matters didn't rest there. Christopher Columbus Gray suddenly did a complete about-face and said that he himself had written the message found in the first bottle.

Although the authorities accepted his word, Mrs. Wormwell refused to believe him. She pointed out the fact that three handwriting experts had all agreed that the message in the bottle found by Gray had been written by the *Deering*'s engineer. It couldn't possibly have been faked.

Unfortunately, her words fell on deaf ears. The government dismissed both messages as hoaxes and the case was closed.

The once-proud *Carroll A. Deering* could not be moved from the spot where she had run aground. After her owners had stripped her of everything of value, she was left to the winds and the waves.

A severe storm struck the Atlantic Coast a few months later. Huge breakers and howling winds battered her. She creaked and groaned in her last great struggle. Then she began breaking up. The storm died before morning, but broken and scattered timbers were all that remained. The *Carroll A. Deering* was no more.

The mystery of what happened to the men who last sailed on her is still unsolved.

IX

A Survivor Tells His Story

Nobody knows exactly how many planes have disappeared without a trace in the Devil's Triangle. It's fairly certain, though, that only one man has gone through two terrifying and unexplained experiences in the Triangle and lived to tell about them. That man is Dick Stern of Atlanta, Georgia.

Mr. Stern was in the Air Force during World War II. In December of 1944, he left the United States for Italy. There were seven bombers in the flight and they all stopped on Bermuda to refuel and rest.

The weather was beautiful when they left the island. A full moon was shining and the night was bright with stars. Conditions couldn't possibly have been better.

Bermuda was only an hour behind them when everything suddenly went wrong. The heavy bomber Stern was in was flipped over onto its back and went completely out of control. The pilot and co-pilot were strapped in their seats, but the other nine men found themselves on the ceiling.

The plane was hurled back and forth and up and down at an incredible rate of speed. The men who weren't wearing their safety belts were thrown around like balls. They were on

A Survivor Tells His Story

the ceiling one second and pinned to the floor the next. Everything in the plane was flying wildly about.

Both the pilot and co-pilot fought furiously for altitude. They were big powerful men and they pulled and heaved at the wheels with all their combined strength. The cold green waters of the Atlantic were coming closer and closer, but the mysterious force refused to let them go.

They were saved by a miracle. The plane was so close to the water that the propellers were churning up whitecaps. Death was staring them in the face. Only at the last possible second did they finally fight free of the unknown force that had been trying to destroy them. The big bomber came out of its diving somersault, leveled off, and slowly began its climb back up into the sky.

The men were in no condition to continue the flight. They had undergone a terrifying experience and needed time to recover. The pilot banked the plane and set his course for Bermuda. As soon as they landed, they were given some bad news. Five of the seven bombers that had left the island only a little more than an hour earlier had been lost at sea. None of them had even radioed in a distress call.

An intense search for the five missing bombers produced nothing. Neither could anything be learned from the pilots of the two planes that had managed to get safely back to Bermuda. They simply did not know what had happened to them. Their planes had flown into a strange force. Was it a known phenomenon such as *clear air turbulence*? It was impossible to know.

Military authorities were completely confused. They had no idea at all as to what had happened. The entire thing defied explanation. It couldn't have been the weather because the night had been bright and starry. Pilot error could be dismissed because seven pilots certainly wouldn't all make the same mistake at the same time. Mechanical difficulties could also be ruled out. Something had caused seven big bombers to go out of control, but nobody knew what that mysterious and deadly something could be. The investigators closed their files and the two planes and crews again took off for Italy.

Although the flight to Europe was uneventful, the Devil's Triangle still wasn't through with Dick Stern. Seventeen years later, he and his wife were on a flight from London, England, to Miami, Florida. They were traveling on a commercial airliner that was to make scheduled stops at Bermuda and Nassau in the Bahamas.

The weather was fine and a meal was served soon after takeoff from Bermuda. Stern and his wife had met the pilot and he joined them while they were waiting for their lunch.

Stern was telling the pilot about his frightening experience in this same area during the war when he got another fright. The plane suddenly shuddered and shook, then dropped straight down. Food and drink on the trays were thrown to the ceiling. Passengers screamed and caught hold of anything they could hang on to. The pilot fought his way back to the cockpit as swiftly as he could.

The smooth flight had become a hideous nightmare. Food, drink, coats, luggage, and a host of other things were strewn throughout the cabin. There was nothing the airline stewardesses could do to help the terrified passengers. They needed all of their strength to keep from being thrown out of their seats.

There were no outward signs of panic in the cockpit. The pilots had been trained to keep calm in any emergency. The lives of their passengers were their first concern and they fought desperately to keep the plane on a level course.

This was a terribly difficult thing to do. The Bristol Britannia aircraft was tossed back and forth and up and down. There was no way to bring it under control. It was as helpless as a leaf in a whirlwind, but the crew couldn't imagine why. There didn't seem to be any turbulence of any kind. Neither were there any threatening clouds in their flight path. The same unknown force that Dick Stern had experienced seventeen years ago was again at work. An unknown and unseen something was trying to drag the plane out of the sky.

The frightening ordeal went on for fifteen terror-filled minutes. Then it ended as suddenly as it had begun. The violent turbulence subsided in a split second and the rest of the flight to the Bahamas was smooth and uneventful. Several of the passengers and crew, however, had to be treated for shock.

Dick Stern made it safely back home. He had survived two terrible experiences in the Devil's Triangle and had no wish to fly through the region again.

The *Star Tiger*

British South American Airways Corporation was formed in 1946, just a year after the end of World War II. It's a long way from England to the bottom of the South American continent. Planes capable of flying great distances were needed, so the company purchased several huge, four-engined Avro Tudors. These could carry enough fuel to stay aloft for sixteen hours.

The men who flew for British South American were all highly experienced. They had flown against the enemy during the war and none of them had less than 1,500 hours of flying time. Brian McMillan, the thirty-four-year-old captain of the *Star Tiger*, had spent well over 3,000 hours piloting planes of various kinds.

The *Star Tiger* was scheduled to leave London Airport on January 27, 1948. There were five other crew members besides Captain McMillan. First Officer David Colby and Second Officer Cyril Ellison had both been pilots in the Royal Air Force. Robert Tuck, the radio officer, was reported to be the very best man in the business. The two air hostesses, known as "Star Girls," were Lynn Clayton and Sheila Nicholls. Miss

Clayton had survived a terrible plane crash in West Africa only nine months earlier.

One of the most distinguished passengers on the *Star Tiger*'s flight was Major Alexander "Sandy" Bardwell. During the war, he had been decorated several times for outstanding courage on the field of battle. He was wounded and taken prisoner on the Greek island of Crete. Soon after being liberated, he went to Palestine as second in command of the First Argyll Regiment. He got married while home on leave from the Middle East and was taking his new bride to the romantic island of Bermuda for their honeymoon.

Bardwell is a well-known name in the lovely, lonely hills and lakes of Argyll, Scotland. It is said in Argyll that the eldest son in a Bardwell family never dies in bed. He always dies a violent death. This has been true for many generations. A number of eldest sons have been killed in battle. The others died of different causes, but all of them died violently. This unfortunate tradition was also to hold true in the case of Major "Sandy" Bardwell.

Conditions on board the *Star Tiger* between London and Lisbon, Portugal, were dreadful. The heating system broke down soon after takeoff and the cold was agonizing. Icicles formed on the roof of the cabin. The inside windows were covered with frost and it was impossible to see out. The passengers shivered miserably in their seats, but nothing could be done.

Lisbon, fortunately, was warm and sunny. The passengers spent a comfortable night in a hotel, then reported back to the airport at eight o'clock in the morning. Mechanics had repaired the heating system and takeoff was scheduled for nine o'clock. Captain McMillan, however, was not satisfied with the performance of one of his engines. The mechanics soon found out what was wrong and the *Star Tiger* took off for the Azores a few minutes before noon.

McMillan's troubles were far from over. As soon as the

plane reached its cruising altitude of 21,000 feet, the heating system again broke down. Icicles formed on the ceiling and once more the windows frosted over. The only thing that cheered the passengers was the belief that they would be in sunny Bermuda in the morning.

But there were still more problems to come. A gale-force wind was howling across the runway when Captain McMillan landed on the island of Santa Maria in the Azores. This was a matter that required some serious thought. He had planned to take off immediately after refueling. Planes bound for Bermuda always took off from the Azores in the afternoon and flew through the night.

The weather report from the meteorological office was far from encouraging. Clouds and strong winds could be expected for the first thousand miles. This was the sort of news that the crew didn't want to hear. If the skies were overcast, it would not be possible for the navigator to plot their position by the stars. Bermuda was about 2,000 miles away. The strong winds meant more fuel consumption and that was an added danger.

Captain McMillan shook his head sadly. The risk was simply not worth taking. Passengers were told that there would be a twenty-four-hour delay. The luggage was unloaded and everyone checked in at the airport hotel.

The weather was much better the next day. There would be moderate headwinds and some overcast, but this wasn't really serious. McMillan decided that no further delay was necessary. They would take off for Bermuda at half past three in the afternoon.

But now another problem popped up. With full fuel tanks and twenty-five passengers on board, the Tudor would be carrying more weight than the safety regulations allowed. This was truly a tough one and McMillan wasn't sure whether to leave some passengers behind or to reduce his fuel load.

He didn't like the idea of leaving two or three passengers in the Azores. The flight had been very uncomfortable so far and there had already been two delays. He just couldn't ask anyone to wait there until the next British South American Airways plane arrived from London.

Neither did Captain McMillan like the idea of taking off with a reduced fuel load. It was a long way to Bermuda and every gallon counted. The headwinds increased fuel consumption and it would be sheer idiocy to leave without full tanks. It was only on the Azores-Bermuda leg of the flight that Tudors took off with their tanks full.

Although he knew that there was a slight risk involved, the pilot asked the traffic assistant to fill his tanks right up to the top. Most of the overweight would be used up while taxiing down the field and in the takeoff run, he reasoned. He also rejected the idea of leaving any passengers behind. They were all anxious to see Bermuda and it was his job to get them there.

At 3:30 P.M., January 29, 1948, the *Star Tiger* left the airport of Santa Maria in the Azores. Her next destination was Bermuda.

There was enough fuel in the tanks to keep the Tudor aloft for sixteen hours. Captain McMillan estimated the flying time to Bermuda at just slightly over 12 hours. Unless something unforeseen happened, there would still be plenty of gas left when they landed.

The poor passengers were in for a bad time of it. They had been freezing in their seats from London all the way to the Azores. Now it was warm enough, but the plane pitched and bucked like a wild pony. Nobody felt like eating and quite a few people were violently airsick.

Business in the cockpit went on in a brisk and efficient manner. There was no time to relax on this leg of the flight. They were flying at an altitude of only 2,000 feet and could easily see the storm-tossed Atlantic beneath them.

Turbulence became more severe after dark. The strength of the headwinds increased and so did the discomfort of the

A British South American Airways Avro Tudor IV. Two identical planes, the *Star Tiger* and the *Star Ariel*, vanished near Bermuda.

passengers. Hardly anyone was able to get any sleep. Although Captain McMillan knew that they would not arrive in Bermuda at the scheduled time, he wasn't worried. The plane was performing well and there was a promise of better weather ahead.

Twelve hours after leaving the Azores, the *Star Tiger* made radio contact with Bermuda. Robert Tuck, the radio officer, asked for a bearing and was told that the plane was right on course. Tuck and McMillan grinned at one another. A series of these bearings would guide them safely to the island.

The tough part of the flight was over. They were almost home.

The ground operator on Bermuda waited for further word from the *Star Tiger*. It was approaching the island and it seemed strange that there had been no more requests for bearings. When he tried to make contact with the plane, however, there was no reply. He kept trying, but his calls were not answered. Something had happened to the *Star Tiger* and the ground operator raised the alarm 95 minutes after the last contact.

British planes and the American Search and Rescue Mission at Kindley Field were out over the Atlantic at the crack of dawn. One of the aircraft was a Flying Fortress with a radar scanner. The search was concentrated on the area between Bermuda and the point from which Robert Tuck had requested a bearing from Bermuda.

The planes were in the air from dawn to dusk. After five long days, the search was finally called off. Not a single thing had been found. No wreckage, no oil slick, no survivors. Nothing.

Nor was anything learned during the course of the investigation that followed. Aeronautical engineers stressed the fact that the Tudors were extremely well made aircraft. Loss of pilot control was ruled out because either McMillan, Colby, or Ellison could have brought the plane into Bermuda.

Radio failure also seemed improbable. The *Star Tiger* carried the best radio aids available. It was highly unlikely that these could have failed. There was one question, though, that couldn't be answered. If the plane had been in trouble, why hadn't the radio officer sent out a distress signal? Robert Tuck was a skilled and experienced operator. If he had so much as touched the transmitting key, some station would surely have heard him.

Why, then, hadn't he done it? Had the plane been destroyed so quickly that there hadn't even been time enough for that?

These were questions that the investigators couldn't

answer. Nor could anyone else. Nobody knew what had happened to the *Star Tiger*, but many believed that she had been destroyed or swallowed up by some mysterious and unknown force.

The disappearance of the British South American Airways plane added one more chapter to the book of Bardwell tragedies and another to the tragedies of the Devil's Triangle.

XI

Other Mysteries of the Air

In 1948, the same year in which the *Star Tiger* vanished, another commercial airliner disappeared without trace in the Devil's Triangle. The plane was a DC-3, one of the most rugged and reliable aircraft ever built.

It was exactly 10:03 P.M. on the second day after Christmas when the plane took off from the airport of San Juan, Puerto Rico. Her destination was Miami, Florida. The distance was roughly 1,200 miles and there would be no stops en route.

The twenty-seven passengers on board the plane were all young Puerto Ricans. They had flown home to their native island for the Christmas holidays and were now returning to their jobs. Everyone was in a happy mood. Some passengers were singing Christmas carols; others were telling about their experiences at home.

Mary Burke, a stewardess from Jersey City, New Jersey, turned the overhead lights off shortly after midnight. The passengers made themselves as comfortable as possible and tried to get some sleep. They were due to arrive in Miami at 4:30 A.M. Some of them had to go to work soon after arrival and they needed all the rest they could get.

Things in the cockpit were going along smoothly. The weather was perfect and the DC-3 was a very easy plane to fly. Captain Bob Linquist and co-pilot Ernest Hill, both from Florida, looked out at the bright stars twinkling in the sky. A few scattered clouds drifted high above them. The scene was one of peace and beauty.

Captain Linquist radioed a position report at quarter past four. They were about fifty miles south of Miami, he reported, and all was well.

But when the tower tried to contact the aircraft, there was no reply! This seemed very strange indeed. Captain Linquist was an experienced pilot. He certainly wouldn't attempt a landing without directions from the tower.

A thoroughly puzzled radio operator made every effort to reach the DC-3. Other stations also tried to make contact, but they had no luck. They were finally forced to admit that something had gone wrong. The alarm was sounded and the search got underway immediately.

It simply never occurred to anyone that they might have trouble finding the missing plane. It had disappeared so close to the mainland that the pilot had probably been able to see the lights of Miami. Besides, conditions for the search were close to perfect. The sea was so shallow and the water so clear that it should have been easy to spot anything as large as the DC-3. If sharks and barracuda had found the people on board the plane, these could also be seen from the air.

Ships and planes from the Air Force, Navy, and Coast Guard hurried to the aircraft's last reported position. From there, they fanned out in all directions. Everyone was optimistic. Finding the plane should present no problems whatsoever. Even if they didn't find the passengers and crew huddled together on life rafts, they would at least find wreckage or an oil slick.

The optimism was short-lived. Planes flying almost wing tip to wing tip crossed and crisscrossed the area and found nothing. Neither did the fleet of ships that was combing the seas nor the men who were searching the land.

Officials refused to accept the fact that the missing DC-3 could not be found. This was their chance to solve the deadly mystery of the Devil's Triangle and they weren't going to miss it. There had to be some explanation for the loss of so many ships and planes. The DC-3 might give them some answers, so they had to keep on looking.

The search was intensified. Men and machines fought their way through the dreary swamps of the Everglades. Planes and ships scoured the Atlantic, the Caribbean, and the Gulf of Mexico. They went as far north as the Carolinas and as far south as Cuba. And they found nothing! They found absolutely nothing. Three hundred thousand square miles of land and sea had been gone over practically inch by inch and not so much as one sliver of debris had been found. Instead of giving up the search after the customary five days, the hunt went on until January 10—two full weeks after the date of the plane's disappearance. Not until then was the search finally called off.

What had happened? What was this strange force that had snatched a large plane right out of the sky? How could an aircraft possibly disappear without trace on its approach to the airfield? What terrible fate had wiped out the thirty-two people on board? What mysterious power had struck so swiftly that the pilot didn't even have enough time to snap the switch that would automatically have sent out a distress call? How could one of the most intensive searches ever launched produce nothing?

These questions and many others were asked by thousands of people.

So far, not a single one of them has been answered.

Exactly one week after the search for the DC-3 was called off, the deadly jinx of the Devil's Triangle struck again. The victim this time was the *Star Ariel*, sister plane of the *Star Tiger*, which had disappeared less than a year before.

On January 17, 1949, the *Star Ariel* landed on Bermuda after an uneventful flight from London. Her ultimate destination was Santiago, Chile. The next leg of her journey was Kingston, Jamaica. Although the flying time to Jamaica was only 5½ hours, sufficient fuel for ten hours of flight was in the tanks. The flight to Kingston was entirely within the Devil's Triangle and the extra fuel was perhaps an added precaution.

Captain J. C. McPhee, a veteran pilot of many transatlantic crossings, was in command of the large four-engine Tudor. There were six crew members on board and twelve passengers. The skies were clear and the seas were calm when the plane took off from Bermuda at 8:45 A.M.

An hour after takeoff, Captain McPhee contacted Bermuda Radio Control. The weather was fine and all was well, he reported. He then added that he was changing radio frequency to make contact with Jamaica Radio Control. This was the last word ever heard from the *Star Ariel.*

British South American Airways operators tried in vain to make contact with the aircraft. There had been no distress signal and no hint of trouble, so they weren't unduly concerned. Flying conditions were perfect. Mechanics on Bermuda had checked the Tudor and pronounced her to be in excellent shape. There seemed to be no reason to worry.

The alarm wasn't sounded until after four long hours of radio silence. Air-Sea Rescue was alerted and planes were ready to take off at a moment's notice. The search didn't really get underway, however, until the *Star Ariel* failed to arrive on schedule. It was only then that people were forced to admit that another large plane had vanished mysteriously in the Devil's Triangle.

At the time of the *Star Ariel*'s disappearance, there were a large number of United States naval vessels on maneuvers between Bermuda and Jamaica. They now had the perfect opportunity to solve the mystery of the Atlantic's Triangle of Death. If they could find the missing plane, they might be able to discover what had happened to all the ships and other aircraft that had disappeared in this area.

The search for the *Star Ariel* was on a massive scale.

Military and government officials were absolutely determined to find her. They might have failed to find the DC-3 that had disappeared on her approach to Miami, but they weren't going to fail this time. No effort and no expense would be spared.

One of the largest military operations in peacetime history went into swift and concerted action. Dozens of planes roared off from the decks of the aircraft carriers *Kearsarge* and *Leyte*. The mighty battleship *Missouri* steamed toward the area in the company of six destroyers. Merchant vessels and commercial airliners traveling anywhere near Jamaica or Bermuda were asked to be on the lookout.

Every available plane was pressed into the search. They came from Bermuda, Jamaica, Cuba, and the Bahamas. Coast Guard stations sent word that aircraft from New York City, Salem, Massachusetts, and Elizabeth City, North Carolina, were ready to leave for Bermuda. Navy and Air Force planes were placed on the alert. If the *Star Ariel* wasn't found soon, they would also take part in the search mission.

By the morning of January 18, a large number of ships, nearly a hundred search planes, and approximately 13,000 men were scouring the sea in search of the missing airliner.

It was almost ridiculous to think that the mission could fail.

A report from a United States bomber pilot caused a flurry of excitement at Air-Sea Rescue headquarters. The pilot stated that he had seen a strange light on the sea before dawn on January 18. He gave the position as roughly 300 miles south of Bermuda. Not knowing that a plane had disappeared somewhere in the area, he didn't give the matter much thought at the time.

This was a report of great significance. The *Star Ariel* would have run out of fuel early in the evening of January 17 and might have ditched at sea. It was quite likely, therefore, that the strange light had come from one of the life rafts.

Planes and destroyers were immediately rushed to the

position reported by the bomber pilot. They searched the area for two full days with painstaking thoroughness—and found nothing.

Another report came in on January 20. This one was from the pilot of a British South American Airways Constellation. He, too, had seen a strange light on the water in the predawn darkness. The location was almost exactly the same as that given by the bomber pilot.

Once again ships and planes were ordered to proceed to the spot where the strange light had been sighted. And once again nothing at all was found. The source of the light has never been explained.

On the afternoon of January 22, the last bubble of hope burst. A search plane spotted a yellow object floating close to the route flown by the *Star Ariel*. Its precise position was given and a destroyer fished it out of the sea. The yellow object turned out to be a large empty box that could not possibly have come from the lost aircraft.

Although the gigantic search was called off after a week, the investigation went on for nearly a year. It uncovered no evidence of what might have happened. Officials could only agree that whatever had occurred had happened so fast that there hadn't even been enough time to touch the switch that would have sent out an emergency distress call.

In his summary, the Chief Inspector of Accidents stated, "Through lack of evidence due to no wreckage having been found, the cause of the accident to the *Star Ariel* is unknown.

"The *Star Ariel* was lost almost exactly a year after her sister aircraft, the *Star Tiger*, had disappeared in much the same area in equally mysterious circumstances."

The tragic loss of lives in the Atlantic's Triangle of Death was increasing at an alarming rate.

British South American Airways had a short and unhappy life. In just over two years, the company lost three large planes. Two of them, the *Star Tiger* and the *Star Ariel*, vanished without a trace in the Bermuda Triangle. The third one, the *Star Dust*, did not disappear in the same area. Her disappearance, however, is one of the greatest unsolved mysteries of the air.

The *Star Dust* was due to land at the Santiago, Chile, airport at 5:45 P.M. on August 2, 1947. Exactly four minutes before that, Captain R. J. Cook contacted tower control and said that he would be arriving right on schedule. There was a brief pause, then the single word *stendec* came over the air in a loud and clear voice.

The puzzled radio operator couldn't imagine what the word meant and asked the pilot to repeat it.

"Stendec," said the loud, clear voice. "Stendec."

And then silence!

The *Star Dust* was never heard from again. It vanished within less than four minutes' flying time of a large city and an international airport. Although it seems absolutely impossible, not one single bit of wreckage was ever found.

Nor has anyone ever been able to explain the meaning of the strange word *stendec.*

The loss of three planes with crews and passengers was a blow from which British South American Airways never recovered. It was only a small company and it was financially crippled by the mysterious disappearances.

A year after the loss of the *Star Ariel*, the company was taken over by the British Overseas Airways Corporation.

Bad luck continued to strike down British planes flying over the Devil's Triangle. No reason for the losses was ever learned. There was never any wreckage, any survivors, or clues of any kind. In one case, however, there was the beginning of a distress call.

On February 2, 1953, a British York transport was en route to Jamaica. There were thirty-three passengers and a crew of six on board. Suddenly the men in Radio Control were snapped into rigid attention. Someone had begun to send an SOS. There was no doubt in anyone's mind about that. Strangely, though, the distress call was never completed.

This was truly a strange turn of events and could mean only one thing: The transport had been struck so severely and so suddenly that there hadn't even been enough time to complete the call for help. Whatever it was that had happened must have happened in a split second.

This time the searchers knew almost exactly where to start looking. They had the transport's last position and expected to find it with no trouble. Planes and ships hurried to the location and scoured the sea. Five days later, they reluctantly gave up the search. The transport and the thirty-nine people on board had been completely swallowed up by the Devil's Triangle.

The United States Naval Air Force has also been plagued by mysterious disappearances in the Atlantic's Triangle of Death. The best-known case, of course, is the loss of the five Avenger bombers of Flight 19 and the huge Martin Mariner flying boat that vanished while searching for them. Twenty-seven lives were lost on that unfortunate day, but nine years later an even more tragic loss was suffered.

On October 30, 1954, forty-two people boarded a four-engine Navy Super-Constellation for a flight to the Azores. Four Navy wives and five children were among the passengers. The plane developed mechanical trouble two and a half hours after takeoff and the pilot returned to base. At 9:39 that night, the crew and passengers were back in the air in another Super-Constellation.

The first position report was received at the scheduled time. It was customary for the pilot to make contact with the shore at hourly intervals, but not another word was heard from the big transport after its first report. Every effort to contact the plane was greeted by complete radio silence. Something had gone wrong and the alarm was sounded an hour after midnight.

Time was vitally important and not a moment was lost.

Other Mysteries of the Air 101

Planes and ships equipped with special radar for night operations took off immediately. Others joined the search at dawn. They came from Bermuda, the Azores, and from bases up and down the Atlantic coast. Forty-two lives were at stake and no effort was spared.

In spite of the evil reputation of the Devil's Triangle, the searchers were confident of success. If the Super-Constellation had ditched at sea, it could stay afloat for many hours. There were plenty of life rafts and life jackets on board and everyone should have a fairly good chance of surviving. Even bad weather wouldn't be a serious problem. The plane carried ninety exposure suits and these would keep the survivors warm and dry.

The search was spread out over nearly a million square miles of the Atlantic. It stretched from the eastern seaboard of the United States to the Azores. The flight plan of the missing plane was studied carefully and most of the activity was concentrated in a path 120 miles wide that followed the proposed course of the Constellation.

Nothing was left to chance. The entire operation was carried out in a thoroughly scientific manner. Every report of anything unusual was checked at once. Every square yard of the mammoth search area was checked every six hours. Over 200 planes and thirty ships were on the lookout at all hours. If there was even one scrap of evidence floating around anywhere in that vast expanse of ocean, it would almost certainly be found.

But the search was an utter and complete failure. High hopes waned and a feeling of despair set in. Crews on the ships and planes had reached the point of total exhaustion. All of them were beginning to believe that they were searching for something that no longer existed. The mysterious force that haunted the Devil's Triangle still refused to give up its deadly secrets.

After eight days of intensive nonstop searching, the operation was finally called off. A jinx that nobody could explain had claimed another large plane and the forty-two people on board her.

"There is no longer any hope of finding some physical clue to the cause of this tragic event," declared a Navy spokesman.

A United States Navy plane was again reported missing in the Devil's Triangle on November 9, 1956. This time it was a twin-engine Martin Marlin P5M Patrol Bomber. There were ten crew members on board when she left the naval station on Bermuda.

The first position report radioed in at 8:30 P.M. was strictly routine. Weather conditions were favorable and the plane was 350 miles from home base. That was the only report received and a search by ships and aircraft was ordered after three hours of radio silence.

For once, there didn't seem to be any great hurry. After all, the missing aircraft was a seaplane. If it had developed mechanical difficulties, the pilot would simply put it down on the ocean and wait for someone to come along on a rescue mission.

There was, however, one disturbing question: The flying boat had two transmitters, so why hadn't there been a distress call? The same thing had happened in the case of other planes and the mystery was still unsolved. Now, though, it seemed likely that the answer to that problem could be found. Once the missing seaplane had been located, the pilot could fill them in on all the details.

Several strange things happened during the course of the search. The mission had scarcely gotten underway when a message was received from the Liberian freighter *Captain Lyras*. It stated that crew members had seen a plane in flames over the Atlantic at about 9:15 P.M. The position given was close to the estimated position of the seaplane at that time.

Coast Guard and Navy aircraft, two destroyers and a light cutter left for the area immediately. While on their way, another message came in from the *Captain Lyras*. She radioed Air-Sea Rescue headquarters that she had sighted what appeared to be a life raft with a light on it. The object was roughly four miles from the freighter. They had lost sight of it in the darkness, but the entire crew was on deck keeping a sharp lookout.

Excitement ran high. The search planes reached the area in less than two hours. Flares were dropped and brilliant light flooded many square miles of the Atlantic. Flying boats from Bermuda flew low over the sea in a wing tip to wing tip search. The destroyers and cutter arrived the following morning. Visibility was good. The position of the missing plane had been pinpointed. If anything was out there, they'd be sure to find it.

But they didn't! To the utter amazement and great disappointment of the search and rescue mission, nothing whatsoever was found. It was the same old story all over again. There had been no distress signal from the missing plane. Neither was there a single survivor or a single piece of wreckage to tell the story of what had happened.

Then another piece was suddenly added to the puzzle. A ship reported that it had flashed a powerful searchlight on a plane flying low overhead. The plane, however, was not in any trouble.

Investigations showed that this ship and the *Captain Lyras* had been in the same vicinity at the time. Wasn't it possible, then, that the crew of the *Captain Lyras* had seen the searchlight flashed on the plane and mistakenly concluded that the aircraft was on fire?

This was possible, it's true, but it still left some questions unanswered. What, for example, was the object that the men on the Liberian freighter had thought was a life raft with a light on it? Where had it come from and how did it disappear? The freighter crew had seen it, but there was no sign of it when the search and rescue team arrived on the scene.

The entire incident now became a mystery within a mystery. If the seaplane had not been in any trouble when the ship flashed the searchlight on it, then it meant that it could have flown on for an indefinite length of time. And that meant that it might have disappeared ten minutes later or several hours later. This was something that nobody would ever know.

After five days and nights of constant searching, the ships and planes were called home. It was an anguishing decision. Finding the missing seaplane might have furnished some clue, but the Devil's Triangle was still stubbornly refusing to give up any of its secrets.

The U.S. Air Force vs. the Devil's Triangle

Although no American airlines have lost any passenger planes in the Atlantic's Triangle of Death, the United States Air Force has had a number of unexplained and almost unbelievable disappearances.

On January 8, 1962, a KB-50 tanker with nine men on board vanished without a trace while on a flight to the Azores. On August 28, 1963, two KC-135 Stratotankers were lost on a routine flight between Bermuda and the Bahamas. Search planes found wreckage near the tankers' last reported position and it was assumed that they had collided.

Two days later, however, more wreckage was found nearly 200 miles to the south. This presented a very curious problem indeed. Investigators knew only too well that planes and ships normally vanished without a trace in the Devil's Triangle. In this case, though, debris had been found, but the mystery remained. There was no clue as to why the planes had crashed. Neither was it possible to learn why there had been no distress signals.

One Air Force official stated his belief that the men in both planes had been dead or unconscious *before* they plunged into the sea. He suggested that the oxygen system may have failed or that some "unexplained force" may have killed the crews. Another official insists that there was a midair collision, but the Air Force says that the two planes were in radio contact with one another and not flying close together.

On September 22, 1963, less than a month after the unfortunate incident involving the loss of the Stratotankers, the Air Force was dealt another blow. A C-133 Cargomaster with a crew of ten disappeared into the unknown. She was on her way to the Azores when she was struck down. There were no distress signals and no hint of trouble. The planes and ships that searched for her came home empty-handed.

The next three Air Force planes to disappear in the Devil's Triangle did so under the most mysterious circumstances imaginable. One was a C-119 cargo plane known as the "Flying Boxcar."

Major Louis Giuntoli of New York was at the controls when the giant aircraft took off from Florida's Homestead Air Force Base on June 5, 1965. Her destination was Grand Turk Island in the Bahamas. There were ten men on board the plane.

The weather was fine and the plane headed southeast into the Devil's Triangle. Everything was strictly routine until the C-119 made her approach to Grand Turk. Then the men in tower control picked up a strange message that they couldn't understand. It made no sense whatsoever and they asked that it be repeated.

But not another word came from the Flying Boxcar. Every attempt to contact her failed completely. The alarm was sounded and the ships and planes set out as soon as possible. If the C-119 had kept to her course, they'd find her with no trouble. She was big and slow, so she had to be somewhere in the immediate vicinity of the island.

The search produced nothing but dashed hopes. Everyone knew that a large plane could not suddenly disappear without a trace while making an approach to an airfield; yet that was precisely what had happened.

Homestead Air Force Base was also the takeoff point for another plane that set out on a journey of no return. The date was September 10, 1971. Captain John Romero of Lafayette, Louisiana, and Lieutenant Norman Northrup of Portland, Oregon, were in the cockpit of the Phantom jet fighter when it zoomed out over the Atlantic. Four technicians tracked its flight on radar.

While the men were watching, the jet suddenly disappeared from the radar screen. They had trouble believing their own eyes. It had happened so fast that it took them a minute or two to realize what had happened. Then the alarm was sounded. Within minutes, other jets were swooping over the area where the Phantom fighter had disappeared.

Everything seemed to be in favor of those searching for the missing plane. They could pinpoint the exact spot where it had last been observed on the radar screen. It was still early in the morning. Visibility was perfect and the jet had disappeared over the Great Bahama Bank. The water was clear and only about ten to twenty feet deep, so they could easily see a plane lying on the bottom.

Unfortunately, however, the searching party didn't see a thing. Tens of thousands of square miles of Florida and Bahama waters were searched thoroughly, but there were no results of any kind.

An even more mysterious incident occurred on October 20, 1971. In this case, the plane disappeared right before the eyes of a group of scientists.

The *Discoverer*, an oceanographic research vessel, was working south of Great Inagua Island in the Bahamas. A four-engine Super-Constellation flew overhead and the men watched it idly. Suddenly, something went wrong! The plane literally stopped in its tracks, then plummeted straight down into the sea.

It only took the *Discoverer* a matter of minutes to reach the scene of the crash. To the absolute amazement of the scientists, there was nothing to be seen. The terrific impact must have smashed the plane to bits, but not one scrap of wreckage floated to the surface. There wasn't even any indication of an oil slick. Although the research vessel carried the most modern and sophisticated detecting equipment, it was unable to find any trace of the plane.

The scientists looked at one another and shook their heads. It was easier to believe that the Super-Constellation had never even existed than to believe that it could have vanished so completely.

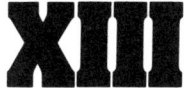

Questions Still Unanswered

Scientists are intensely eager to solve the mystery of the Devil's Triangle for once and always. They want to find out just exactly what strange and mysterious forces are responsible for the many unexplained tragedies that have occurred in that area.

The majority of the theories advanced so far are either too simple or too far-fetched to be considered seriously. It's ridiculous to suppose, for example, that a giant octopus dragged the *Cyclops* down to the bottom. After all, the *Cyclops* was a 19,000-ton ship, was nearly 600 feet long, and had 309 men on board. Something very unusual *did* happen to the *Cyclops*, it's true, but there was no octopus involved.

Waterspouts and freak waves can also be ruled out because these would have no effect on an airliner flying at an altitude of 20,000 feet. By the same reasoning, an airplane could crash because of mechanical difficulties, but this couldn't apply to a yacht.

So was the same mysterious force responsible for all of the unexplained disappearances in the Devil's Triangle? Did the strange "something" that destroyed the *Star Tiger* and the *Star Ariel* also destroy the *Cyclops* and the *Proteus*? Is the same force causing the disappearances of both huge aircraft flying high above sea level and small yachts sailing on the sea?

The pattern of disappearances certainly seems to be very much the same. In most cases, there were no distress calls and no indications of trouble. Whatever had happened must have happened very quickly. In many instances, the last reports stated that all was well.

The complete lack of debris also fits the pattern. How could all of the ships and planes have vanished without a trace? How could ships the size of the *Cyclops, Nereus*, and *Proteus* suddenly disappear from the face of the earth? When a ship or plane goes down into the sea, something always comes up. An oil slick, a deck chair, a life raft, or something else always floats to the surface. This is not true in the Devil's Triangle, however, and nobody has yet been able to explain it satisfactorily.

There have, of course, been some attempts. Flying saucer enthusiasts insist that everything has been spirited away to outer space. Some say that people from other worlds have completely disintegrated the ships and planes with powerful ray guns. Others believe that everything has been seized by an advanced civilization living somewhere on the ocean floor. Still others believe that the ships and planes disappeared into another dimension.

Scientists don't take these theories too seriously. They readily admit that there is something very strange going on in the Devil's Triangle, but they reject the idea that the disappearances are in any way connected with men from outer space or an underwater civilization. Such theories are not in keeping with their scientific training.

They are convinced that some as yet unknown natural force is responsible for the disappearances. The cause may be an atmospheric disturbance, a gravitational disturbance, or an electromagnetic disturbance. Or it may be something else. They don't know the answer yet, but they're trying hard to find it.

When that answer has been found, the mystery of the deadly Devil's Triangle will at last be solved.

BIBLIOGRAPHY

MAGAZINES

Brock, Paul. "They Sailed into Oblivion." *Outlook*, April 1971.

Chance, Paul. "Parapsychology Is an Idea Whose Time Has Come." *Psychology Today*, October 1973.

Comella, Tom. "Have UFO's Swallowed Our Aircraft?" *Fate*, May 1961.

Eckert, Allen. "The Mystery of the Lost Patrol." *American Legion Magazine*, April 1962.

Gaddis, Vincent. "The Deadly Bermuda Triangle." *Argosy*, February 1964.

Hicks, John. "Lost in the Twilight Zone." *Florida Magazine*, January 1971.

Lieber, Leslie. "Limbo of Lost Ships." *This Week*, August 4, 1968.

Marx, Robert. "The Bermuda Triangle: Myth or Mystery?" *Argosy*, February 1974.

McDonell, Michael. "Lost Patrol." *UFO Quarterly Review*, July-September 1973.

McDonell, Michael. "The Mystery of Flight 19." *Naval Aviation News*, January 1973.

Sand, George. "Sea Mystery at Our Back Door." *Fate*, October 1962.

Sanderson, Ivan. "The Spreading Mystery of the Bermuda Triangle." *Argosy*, August 1968.

Smith, Marshall. "The Devil's Triangle." *Cosmopolitan*, September 1973.

Snow, Edgar. "The Bermuda Triangle Mystery." *The Boston Sunday Herald-Traveller Magazine*, February 14, 1971.

Soule, Gardner. "What Happened to the Cyclops?" *American Legion Magazine*, January 1963.

Stern, Richard. "Back Talk Section." *Argosy*, May 1964.
Winer, Richard. "The Devil's Triangle." *Miami Herald Tropic Magazine*, November 15, 1974.
Winer, Richard. "Bermuda Triangle—UFO Twilight Zone." *Saga*, August 1972.
Winer, Richard. "The Deadly Bermuda Triangle—Flying Saucer 'Space Warp' Domain?" *Saga*, September 1972.

BOOKS

Barker, Ralph. *Great Mysteries of the Air*. London: Chatto and Windus, 1966.
Berlitz, Charles. *Mysteries from Forgotten Worlds*. Garden City, N.Y.: Doubleday, 1972.
Burgess, Robert. *Sinkings, Salvages and Shipwrecks*. New York: American Heritage Press, 1972.
Chichester, Sir Francis. *Gipsy Moth Circles the World*. London: Hodder and Stoughton, 1967.
Columbus, Christopher. *Journal of First Voyage to America*. New York: Albert and Charles Boni, 1924.
Gaddis, Vincent. *Invisible Horizons*. Philadelphia: Chilton, 1965.
Godwin, John. *This Baffling World*. New York: Bantam, 1973.
Gould, Rupert. *Enigmas*. New York: University Books, 1965.
Hoehling, Adolph. *They Sailed into Oblivion*. New York: Yoseloff, 1959.
Irving, Washington. *History of the Life and Voyages of Christopher Columbus*. Philadelphia: Carey, Lee and Blanchard, 1835. Volume 2
Jeffrey, Adi-Kent. *The Bermuda Triangle*. New Hope, Pa.: New Hope Publishing Company, 1973.
McDonald, Hastings. *The Mary Celeste*. London: Michael Joseph, 1924.
Sanderson, Ivan. *Invisible Residents*. New York: World, 1970.
Slocum, Joshua. *Sailing Alone Around the World*. New York: Century, 1900.
Spencer, John. *Limbo of the Lost*. New York: Bantam, 1974.
Winer, Richard. *The Devil's Triangle*. New York: Bantam, 1974.

INDEX

Alston, Aaron Burr, 33
Alston, Joseph, 32–34
Alston, Theodosia, 32–38
Amazon, 39
Atlantic Mutual Insurance Company, 47–48
Atmospheric disturbance, 110
Avro Tudors, 86, 88, 91
Azores, 16

Bardwell, Alexander (Sandy), 87, 92
Bates, Henry, 80
Bibby, L. H., 74
Blanchford, George, 47, 49
Briggs, Benjamin Spooner, 40, 41, 43–45, 48, 49
Briggs, Mrs. Benjamin Spooner, 40, 43, 45, 48, 49
British South American Airways Corporation, 86, 98, 99
Burack, Dan, 20–22
Burke, Mary, 93
Burr, Aaron, 32–34

C-119 cargo plane (Flying Boxcar), 106–107

C-133 Cargomaster, 106
Callistre, Jean Baptiste, 36–37
Cape Lookout lightship, 79
Captain Lyras, 102, 103
Carroll A. Deering, 76–81
Celestial phenomena, 26–27
Chichester, Sir Francis, 53
Chronometer, 58
Clayton, Lynn, 86, 87
Clear air turbulence, 83
Colby, David, 86, 91
Columbus, Christopher, 23–30
Compass, 28
Cox, Robert F., 5–7
Cyclops, 61–75, 109, 110

DC-3, 93–95
Dei Gratia, 40, 41, 44–47
Deveau, Oliver, 41, 43–47, 49
Dimension, other, 110
Discoverer, 107–108

Electromagnetic disturbance, 111
Ellison, Cyril, 86, 91

Fireballs, 26

Flight 19, 1–15, 100
Flood, Solly, 44–47
Flying saucers, 14, 26, 48, 110
Freak waves, 17, 27, 66, 109

Gaddis, Vincent, 17
Gaines Mills, 10, 11
Gallivan, Robert, 1–3, 5
Giuntoli, Louis, 106
Gottschalk, Alfred, 63
Grand Cayman Island, 59, 60
Gravitational disturbance, 110
Gray, Christopher Columbus, 80–81
Green, Timothy, 34
Gruebel, Robert, 1–3, 5
Gulf Stream, 17
Gypsy Moth, 53

Hamilton, Alexander, 33
Hawes, Dean, 72–75
Hill, Ernest, 94
Horgan, Patrick, 20–22

Jacobson, Thomas, 79
Jeffrey, Walter G., 9, 11

KB-50 tanker, 105
KC-135 Stratotankers, 105
Kearsarge, 97
Kittiwake, 72
Kosnar, Allen, 1–3, 12
Krippner, Stanley, 13–14

Leyte, 97
Liberdade, 56–57
Linquist, Bob, 94
Literary Digest, 66
Livingston, Brockholst, 64

McBean, Alexander, 39–40
McLellan, Charles, 78
McMillan, Brian, 86
McPhee, J. C., 96
Martin Mariner PBM-5 flying boat, 9–12, 26, 100
Martin Marlin P5M Patrol Bomber, 102

Mary Celeste, 39–52
Meteors, 25–26
Missouri, 97
Morehouse, David Reed, 40, 41, 44–47
Mormackite, 27–28
Morrison, J. D., 11, 12

Naval Overseas Transportation Service, 61
Nereus, 68–71, 110
Neutercanes, 27
Nicholls, Sheila, 86
Northrup, Norman, 107

Octopus theory, 66, 109
Opportune, 74
Overstocks, William, 35, 37, 38

Parker, Gilman, 50–52
Patriot, 34–38
Pirates, 30, 36, 37, 80
Powers, Edward J., 5
Proteus, 68–71, 110

Richardson, Albert, 46, 47
Romero, John, 107

Sanderson, Ivan, 17
Sargasso Sea, 23–25
Scorpion, 71–72
Seaweed, 23, 25, 28
Simpson, Joanne, 27
Slocum, Joshua, 53–60
Slocum, Mrs. Joshua, 55, 56
Solomons, 10
Spencer, John Wallace, 16
Spray, 57–60
Star Ariel, 95–99, 110
Star Dust, 99
Star Tiger, 86–92, 98, 110
Stern, Dick, 82–85
Stivers, George, 5
Survey, 62

Taylor, Charles, 3, 5–9, 12

Index

TBM Avenger torpedo bombers, 3–5, 26
Tuck, Robert, 86, 90, 91

UFOs (unidentified flying objects), 14, 26, 48, 110
Underwater civilization, theory of, 110
United States Air Force, 105–108
United States Naval Air Force, 1–15, 100–104
United States Navy Hydrographic Office, 26–27

Valentine, Manson, 13, 14

Venetian, 58
Vengeance, 37
Vortex theory, 13–14

War of 1812, 34–36
Waterspouts, 17, 66, 109
Waves, freak, 17, 27, 66, 109
Whitehurst, William T., 74
Winer, Richard, 17
Witchcraft, 20–22
Worley, George W., 62–68
Worley, Mrs. George W., 68
Wormwell, Willis B., 77–80
Wormwell, Mrs. Willis B., 80–81

ABOUT THE AUTHOR

Elwood D. Baumann was born in Saskatchewan, Canada, and is a graduate of the University of Wisconsin. After many years as a teacher and principal in schools in Venezuela and eastern Turkey, he took up writing as a vocation and travel as an avocation and has now been in one hundred and five countries on six continents.

He has written two other books on the theme of unsolved mysteries of nature—a particular fascination of his. They are *The Loch Ness Monster*, and *Bigfoot: America's Abominable Snowman,* both published by Franklin Watts.